THE POCKET GUIDE TO
FRESHWATER FISHES
OF
BRITAIN AND EUROPE

ALWYNE WHEELER

ILLUSTRATED BY COLIN NEWMAN

**DRAGON'S
WORLD**

Dragon's World Ltd
Limpsfield
Surrey RH8 0DY
Great Britain

First published by Dragon's World 1992

Editor: Diana Payne
Designer: Carole Perks
Art Director: Dave Allen
Editorial Director: Pippa Rubinstein

*The author would like to acknowledge the contribution made to this
book by Mrs Sita Fonseka, who undertook the typing of the
manuscript, and spared no effort to meet the deadline.*

The catalogue record for this book is available from
the British Library

ISBN 1 80528 119 X

Typeset by Dorchester Typesetting, Dorchester

Printed in Singapore

The vast majority of illustrations in this book are in colour.
However, where there is no colour reference available for a
rare, or poorly documented fish, the artist has created black-
and-white line drawing to illustrate the fish as accurately as is
possible without the use of colour.

Contents

Introduction

Freshwater fishes are distributed across the whole of Europe from the Arctic regions of Norway and Sweden to the tip of Spain, and from Ireland eastwards to Greece and Romania. However, they are not evenly spread because both the numbers and kinds of fishes occurring are affected by climate and by the geological history of Europe. Thus, in the Arctic regions very few fish can tolerate the long periods each year in which the surface of the water is frozen, so most of the fish species found there are migratory, entering rivers to breed as soon as the ice breaks and returning to the sea in the autumn. In the Mediterranean countries most of the fish are resident all year round and there are numerous species living in rivers and lakes, although they often face severe droughts caused by human demands for water. Climatic factors, therefore, influence fish distribution and result in an increasing abundance of species as you move from north to south, and similarly from high altitudes to low.

The past history of Europe has been even more influential in affecting fish distribution. The only native fishes in Ireland are those like salmon, eel and stickleback which could colonize the rivers from the sea; other species, such as bream and pike, have been introduced. England has native freshwater fishes in addition to those which have come from the sea. These native fish are believed to have colonized the eastern rivers during the period before the North Sea existed when these rivers were tributaries of the Rhine. The western continental European countries have more species than Britain, most of which colonized their fresh waters from the Rhine following the retreat of the ice after the major ice ages. In turn most of these fish species were derived from the River Danube which has a number of species – such as the huchen and several sturgeons – not found in western Europe.

The freshwater fishes of northern Europe are, geologically speaking, relatively recent immigrants, having spread in the late Pleistocene and more recently along the Danube and the Rhine, while those found in rivers around the Mediterranean basin are much more ancient. Spain, southern France, Italy and the Balkan countries all contain kinds of fish (and many other animals) which differ from those in northern Europe. This is not just a matter of climate; the richness of the fauna is largely due to the escape of much of this region from ice cover during the Pleistocene. Most of the fish species of the northern Mediterranean coastlines are ancient forms which have lived in the region since the Oligocene or Miocene. Some of them are the ancestors of species which survived in the Mediterranean region when it was a freshwater (or slightly saline) inland lake. These fish have lived in the rivers for millions of years, isolated from contact with their relatives once the Mediterranean became salt, and during this period they evolved to form different species. As a result of this the number of fish species found in these Mediterranean countries is often higher than those in northern Europe. This is particularly true of the Balkan countries, Yugoslavia, Albania and Greece, which contain many species which are unique to certain river systems in these areas. Greece has a particularly rich fauna partly due to its many isolated river systems but also because some of the Danubian species have colonized its north-eastern districts.

In addition to the native fishes, a number of exotic fishes have been introduced to Europe, as well as large-scale redistribution of European species. Many of the introductions originated in North America; the rainbow trout is a classic case now found in every European country. Black basses and catfishes have also come from North America, as did the so-called mosquito fish which is abundant in all coastal regions of the Mediterranean.

Redistribution of native fishes has also been widespread. For example, in Ireland no fewer than eight species have been introduced to supplement the six native species. Scotland and Wales have also been stocked with species widespread in England, and England in its turn has received European species, for example, zander, wels catfish, bitterling and carp. Such redistribution of fish is potentially damaging to the native fauna and in parts of southern Europe could be seriously harmful to species which are unique to the river systems.

Introductions of any kind are a form of biological pollution which is likely to have an impact on the native fauna. This is most serious to species which have evolved in isolation, as have many of southern Europe's fishes. Unfortunately this is not the only threat facing them. Pollution of the water is widespread throughout Europe, although varying in its kind from area to area. The obvious crude discharges of industrial effluents, poorly treated or even untreated sewage and farming wastes are all well known and easy to identify. Others such as acid rain and the effects of pesticides are less obvious but none the less just as destructive. Unfortunately they are not confined to the industrialized countries of northern Europe but are developing into potentially serious problems in the Mediterranean countries, which have a richer and more valuable fauna. These countries have also suffered from the tourist industry, in the cause of which wetlands have been drained to build accommodation, which in turn results in pollution by sewage discharges. Perhaps the most serious consequence of these developments is that rivers have been dammed to store water for domestic use as well as to provide power, and in some places this has been done so thoroughly that in the summer season the river bed is dry.

The future prospects are not hopeful for the survival of some of the species which make up the freshwater fish fauna of Europe. Many will survive but these will be mostly the widely distributed species which tolerate poor conditions. The threat is, however, particularly acute in two groups. Migratory fishes require a clear passage along rivers and good quality water in the estuary. The salmon is well known and is now very much scarcer than it once was, but the massive migrations of shads and sturgeons are now virtually extinguished throughout Europe. The other highly threatened group of European fishes occurs in the rivers and coastal wetlands of the Mediterranean basin. These fishes are often represented by small populations, in restricted river systems, and are unique – found nowhere else in the world – but they are seriously under threat. Awareness of their existence and of the threats facing them may help to ensure their continued survival.

ALWYNE WHEELER

Lamprey
Petromyzon marinus

Family name Petromyzontidae (lampreys)
Length 70–90cm (27½–35½in); exceptionally to 1.20m (3ft 11in)
Weight approx. 2.5kg (5lb 8oz)

Identification Eel-like in shape but with a sucker disc. Teeth on sucker disc small at edges, larger, pointed towards centre; tooth plate near oral opening with 7–9 large sharp cusps. Eyes small; seven separate gill openings on each side of head. No true fins (with rays); a fold of skin like a fin near tail and on back. Coloration olive to yellow-brown, heavily blotched with black or dark brown.
Habitat Young lampreys live in fresh water usually buried in silt, often in beds of aquatic plants. These larvae, or 'prides', live in rivers for 6–8 years. They develop into sub-adults which migrate to the sea. Most stay in coastal waters but some have been caught far offshore.
Food Larvae feed by filtering silt and removing diatoms, nematode worms and bacteria from it. Adults are parasites, sucking the blood of bony fishes.
Breeding Adult lampreys return to fresh water in the spring and spawn over gravel shallows in midsummer, in a shallow nest at the top of a riffle and in water about 40–60cm (16–23½in) deep.
Range Coastal regions of Europe and well out into the Atlantic. Breeds in the larger rivers of N. Europe, but is now very rare owing to estuarine pollution and the building of weirs in rivers. A threatened species.

Lampern

Lampetra fluviatilis

Family name Petromyzontidae (lampreys)
Length 50cm (20in)

Identification Eel-like in shape but without pectoral fins, and with 7 gill openings on each side of head. Sucker disc circular but with few distinct, rather blunt teeth. The central tooth plate has 7 cusps. Coloration uniform, the back greeny-brown merging into yellowish sides; cream on the belly.

Habitat Larval lamperns bury themselves in mud and amongst the roots of water plants in rivers. After about 4 years they migrate to the sea, usually in early spring. The adults migrate upstream from the sea in autumn. Adults live in inshore waters.

Food Larvae feed on detritus, algae and diatoms which they filter out of the mud. Adults are parasitic on fishes, mostly members of the herring and cod families, also salmon and smelt. They suck the blood of the host through a wound made by the teeth.

Breeding In spring males hollow out nests in gravel, usually in the upper reaches of rivers, moving the stones with their suckers. Nest is often below a weir or gravel bank but in water to 1.5m (5ft) deep. The eggs are laid in the nest by one or more females.

Range North-western Europe centred on the Baltic, North Sea and Irish Sea basins. Also on the western coast of Italy. Now uncommon in much of Europe owing to pollution of estuaries and the building of weirs and dams.

Brook Lamprey
Lampetra planeri

Family name Petromyzontidae (lampreys)
Length 25cm (9¾in)

Identification Eel-like in shape but without pectoral fins and with 7 gill openings on each side of the head. The dorsal fins are continuous. Sucker disc circular but with small blunt teeth. Dark brown above, sometimes dark grey; yellowish to white ventrally.

Habitat Lives in small streams, usually in the upper reaches of rivers. The larvae burrow in mud and dense weed beds. The adults do not migrate to the sea.

Food Larvae eat diatoms, algae, detritus filtered from the mud. The adults do not feed.

Breeding Larvae mature at about 6–7 years. Spawning occurs in spring in nests made in shallow water, often under bridges or in shade. Usually nests made in sand or gravel areas, but occasionally made in silt provided there are a few pebbles to which the fish can cling. Several lampreys may spawn in the same nest.

Range Northern Europe from Ireland eastwards to the Baltic states and Finland south to central France.

Danubian Lampern

Eudontomyzon danfordi

Family name Petromyzontidae (lampreys)
Length 30cm (12in)

Identification Eel-like but with no pectoral fins and with 7 gill openings on the sides of the head. Teeth on the sucker disc small except for the central area; posterior tooth plate with sharp cusps. Light golden brown on the back fading to yellowish on the belly.

Habitat Lives in small tributaries of part of the Danube. The larvae bury themselves in silt in small brooks where the current is slow. They swim freely at night. At 4–5 years they become adult and move downstream, hiding amongst plant roots in daytime.

Food Larvae eat micro-organisms, worms and insect larvae. The adults are parasites on fishes in the stream, often gnawing into the body cavity of their prey.

Breeding Takes place in spring, the adults are believed to make a nest by removing pebbles and hollowing out the sand.

Range Lives in tributary streams to the Tisza River, a north-bank tributary of the Danube. Its range lies within Slovakia, Romania and western USSR.

Sturgeon

Acipenser sturio

Family name Acipenseridae (sturgeons)
Length 3.5m (11ft 6in); rarely more than 2.5m (8ft 3in)
Weight about 136kg (300lb)

Identification Characteristic body shape with the tail asymmetric and 5 rows of bony plates on back, sides and belly. Snout bluntly pointed; barbels close to mouth, not fringed. 24–40 bony plates in side row. Dark, green-brown above, fading to yellowish on sides and creamy white ventrally.
Habitat Breeds in large rivers, the young stay in fresh water up to 3 years then migrate to the sea. In the river the adults live in the main channel at 2–8m (6ft 6in–26ft) depth, migrating up to 1000km (621 miles) upstream to breed. Young fish stay close to the breeding grounds for a year but slowly drop down the river as they grow.
Food In fresh water the young fish eat small crustaceans, insect larvae and molluscs; the adults probably do not feed.
Breeding Takes place in spring (and summer for northern populations) in deep pools with strong current over pebbles. The eggs are sticky, black, and are quickly buried in the gravel. One female is often accompanied by 2–3 males.
Range Now extremely rare and extinct in many rivers in which it once bred. The only western European river in which it breeds is the Gironde. The land-locked population may still survive in Lake Ladoga. Rarely caught in shallow seas around Europe.

Sterlet
Acipenser rutheneus

Family name Acipenseridae (sturgeons)
Length 1.25m (4ft 1¼in); usually 1.0m (3ft 3in)
Weight 6.0–6.5kg (13lb 4oz–14lb 8oz)

Identification Characteristic body shape with asymmetric tail and 5 rows of bony plates on body. Lateral bony plates numerous, 60–70. Snout long, 4 barbels, fringed on edges. Back dark greyish-brown, yellowish ventrally; the lateral row of scutes is light coloured.
Habitat A riverine fish which is rarely found in reservoirs and large lakes: makes local migrations within the river only. Usually lives close to the river bed in deep water over stony and gravelly bottoms, but after spawning the fish spread out into food-rich sandy and muddy shallows.
Food Bottom-living insect larvae, molluscs, worms and leeches. During spawning season often eats fish eggs, including those of sturgeons.
Breeding In spring when the water level is high, generally between April and mid-June. Most spawn in the river bed in depths of 7–15m (23–50ft), in gravel where the flow is relatively high.
Range Native to the Danube and other tributaries of the Black, Caspian and White Seas. It is now much rarer than it formerly was owing to pollution and alterations in rivers, but is extensively cultivated in lakes within its original range.

Adriatic Sturgeon
Acipenser naccarii

Family name Acipenseridae (sturgeons)
Length 2.0m (6ft 7in)
Weight to 25kg (55lb); usually smaller

Identification Characteristic body shape with asymmetric tail and 5 rows of bony plates on body. Lateral row with 32–42 plates. Snout blunt and rounded, 4 barbels long, their bases nearer tip of snout than mouth. Back dark grey to yellowish; ventrally pale; lateral scutes light.
Habitat Migratory, living in coastal waters in the sea over sandy or muddy bottoms. Enters rivers but seems not to make long migrations in fresh water. Virtually nothing is known of its biology.
Breeding Said to spawn in February and March in shallow, still water near the banks of rivers.
Range Found only in the Adriatic Sea and rivers of N. Italy, Yugoslavia and Albania. The River Po is its stronghold. Is now rare and a threatened species owing to pollution in the sea and in coastal rivers.

Stellate Sturgeon
Acipenser stellatus

Family name Acipenseridae (sturgeons)
Length 2.19m (7ft 2in); usually 1.0–1.20m (3ft 3in–3ft 11in)

Identification Characteristic slender body shape, asymmetrical tail and 5 rows of bony plates on the body. In addition to the major rows of plates there are smaller star-shaped plates in the skin. Snout flattened and long; barbels relatively short. Dark browny-black on back and sides, white ventrally.

Habitat Migratory. Lives in coastal waters of the sea and the lower reaches of rivers. It is an active swimmer and inhabits the middle and upper water layers. Young fish congregate in the estuaries of large rivers.

Food Young fish eat crustaceans, aquatic insect larvae, worms and molluscs; adults eat small fishes while in the sea.

Breeding Spawning takes place in early summer on river banks which are covered by the spring floods, or in the river beds. Eggs are laid on pebbles and gravel bottoms.

Range Lives in the Black Sea and Caspian Sea basins and migrates into those rivers which are not barred by dams or pollution. In the Danube it is confined to the lower part of the river, although it was once much more abundant and widespread.

Beluga
Huso huso

Family name Acipenseridae (sturgeons)
Length reported to 6.0m (19ft 8in)
Weight 1500kg (1½ tons)

Identification Typical sturgeon shape with an asymmetrical tail, but with feeble scutes on back and lower sides only. Mouth wide, virtually across width of head; barbels long, flattened and fringed at their bases. Dull grey on back and sides, lighter ventrally.
Habitat In the sea lives mostly near the surface and in the middle waters over muddy bottoms. Migrates into major rivers to spawn.
Food Young fish in rivers feed on insect larvae and crustaceans, but quickly change to a fish diet. Adults eat a wide range of fishes, water birds and even seals.
Breeding In rivers during spring floods, on hard, stony or gravel bottoms in 4–15m (13–50ft) of water.
Range Lives in the Adriatic, Black Sea and Caspian Sea and the major rivers draining into them. Now extremely rare, on the verge of extinction, in the Adriatic and the River Po. It still occurs in the mouth of the Danube. Throughout its range is less common and less widely distributed than formerly.

Allis Shad
Alosa alosa

Family name Clupeidae (herrings, shads and sprats)
Length 60cm (24in)
Weight 2.7kg (6lb)

Identification Body flattened from side to side with sharp keel on underside, scales forming sharp teeth along belly. Distinct notch in upper jaw. Rakers on first gill arch 80–130, longer than gill filaments. Back deep blue, sides golden, shading to silvery; usually a dusky blotch behind head.
Habitat Migratory, entering large rivers to spawn in spring. Penetrates far up rivers. Occurs in the main channel; adults return to sea after spawning; young fish stay in river and move down to estuary in autumn.
Food Planktonic crustaceans, increasing in size as fish grows. Adults eat small fishes as well as crustaceans.
Breeding Far up rivers at night over gravel where the current is swift; spawning usually in May. The eggs are washed into the gravel; young fish from small schools in the shallows.
Range Western European coasts from Norway south to Morocco and western Mediterranean basin. Enters large rivers within this area to spawn, but now so rare that there are few breeding populations left. A protected species in most European countries.

Twaite Shad
Alosa fallax

Family name Clupeidae (herrings, shads and sprats)
Length 55cm (22in)
Weight 1.5kg (3lb 5oz)

Identification Body flattened from side to side with sharp keel on belly. Distinct notch in upper jaw. Rakers on first gill arch short and thick, 40–60 in number. Back deep blue, sides yellowish, belly silvery-white; a line of dusky blotches along sides.
Habitat Migratory, entering rivers in May–June and spawning near the top of the tidal area. Adults return to the sea; young stay in lower reaches of rivers and drop down to the sea in autumn. Land-locked populations occur in Irish and Italian lakes.
Food Planktonic crustaceans and young fishes.
Breeding Spawns in late spring in fresh water over sand and gravel beds; eggs drop into spaces between gravel.
Range Atlantic coasts of Europe from Iceland, S. Norway to Morocco, the whole of the Mediterranean and S. Black Sea. Enters larger rivers where access is not barred by dams or pollution.

Pontic Shad
Alosa pontica

Family name Clupeidae (herrings, shads and sprats)
Length 45cm (17¾in); usually less

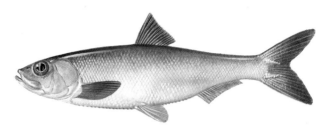

Identification Body slender (more 'herring-like' than 'shad-like'), with toothed scales on belly. Distinct notch in upper jaw. Teeth well developed in jaws. Gill rakers on first arch, thin (about length of gills), 47–69 in number. Blue on back, silvery on sides and belly.
Habitat Migratory; enters rivers flowing into Black Sea in early summer.
Food Mainly small, schooling fishes and crustaceans.
Breeding In rivers, sometimes up to 500km (310 miles) upstream, in summer.
Range Lives in Black Sea and enters northern rivers. Related species live in Caspian Sea, Black Sea and Aegean, some isolated in lakes.

Salmon
Salmo salar

Family name Salmonidae (salmons and trouts)
Length 1.5m (4ft 11in)
Weight up to 36kg (80lb)

Identification Adipose fin present. Caudal peduncle (tail-fin stalk) narrow, the tail-fin rays stand out from the outline above and below; tail fin slightly forked. Upper jawbone extends to the level of the rear of the eye, not beyond. Large fish (adults returning from sea and smolts) are silvery in colour, white beneath, and have small x-shaped spots on the sides. Young fish (parr) are dark above with a series of 8–11 dark, rounded marks on the sides with a single orange spot between these parr marks.
Habitat Salmon parr in shallow water in small streams towards the head waters of rivers. Later they spread out downstream, living close to stones and rocks. Between 1–3 years of age they become silvery smolts, move downstream and eventually out to sea. Adults range widely in the ocean, returning to the river in 1–3 years.
Food Parr eat aquatic insects, crustaceans, and a substantial amount of insects and small animals that drop into the water. In the sea food is mostly crustaceans (shrimps, etc.).
Breeding Spawning takes place upstream in rivers in a nest (redd) made by the female in gravel in November–December. The eggs are buried in the gravel, hatching in early spring.
Range Northern Europe (White Sea to N. Spain), Iceland, off S. Greenland, and the E. coast of North America. Ranges across the Atlantic on feeding migrations. Rarer than formerly owing to pollution, obstructions in rivers and over-fishing.

Trout
Salmo trutta

Family name Salmonidae (salmons and trouts)
Length variable according to habitat; small rivers 30cm
(12in), sea trout 1.4m (4ft 7in)
Weight up to 9.9kg (22lb)

Identification Adipose fin present. Caudal peduncle deep,
flat sided; tail fin rays merge into body outline above and
below. Tail fin usually square cut. Upper jawbone extends past
eye level. Coloration variable, brownish, numerous black spots
on upper sides and rusty red spots; in estuaries and the sea
silvery with sparse dark spots; adipose fin orange edged.
Habitat Lives in small brooks to the largest rivers and lakes.
Migratory form goes to sea to feed. Generally requires clean,
well-oxygenated water. Young trout live close to gravel and
pebbles in shallow water; larger ones tend to lie close to cover,
under overhanging trees, bridges.
Food Trout eat insect larvae and crustaceans, flying aquatic
insects and animals that fall out of overhanging trees. Large
trout are often fish eaters. Food habits are variable; some types
eat aquatic snails.
Breeding Spawning between October and January; eggs laid
in redds made in pea-sized gravel by female. Eggs hatch in 6–8
weeks but stay in the gravel for up to 6 weeks after hatching.
Range In fresh water from N. Norway to Spain (rare) and
Atlas Mountains (possibly extinct), from Ireland to USSR. As
sea trout in coastal waters of N. Europe. Much scarcer than
formerly.

Rainbow Trout
Oncorhynchus mykiss

Family name Salmonidae (salmons and trouts)
Length 1.0m (3ft 3in); migratory form (N. America) larger
Weight up to 11kg (24lb 3oz)

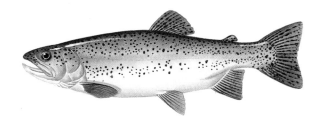

Identification Adipose fin present. Caudal peduncle deep and flat sided; tail fin slightly forked. Scales very small. Coloration distinctive, usually a pinkish-rainbow stripe along sides; dense black spots on back and upper sides, dorsal, adipose and caudal fins.
Habitat A N. American (west coast) fish widely introduced to Europe. Mostly occurs in artificial still waters, reservoirs, lakes and in some rivers. Lives in similar places to brown trout but can tolerate higher temperatures and less clean water.
Food Insects (both aquatic and aerial), crustaceans and fishes (larger specimens only); planktonic crustaceans are important food in still waters.
Breeding Most rainbow trout are raised in hatcheries and then released. A few breeding populations are known. In these hatcheries spawning takes place in early winter in redds dug by the female.
Range Native to western N. America, Mexico to Alaska. Here rainbow trout live in small streams, 'kamloops' live in deep cool lakes, and 'steelhead' are migratory to the sea. The fish farm stocks are mostly rainbow, but some mixing has taken place.

'Adriatic Trout'
Salmothymus obtusirostris

Family name Salmonidae (salmons and trouts)
Length 50cm (20in); usually up to 25cm (9¾in)

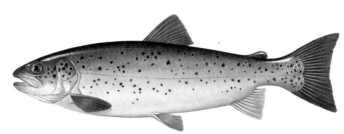

Identification Trout-like in appearance with an adipose fin, narrow caudal peduncle and forked tail fin. The head is distinctly shorter than in brown trout and the snout is blunt. Back greenish-brown with sparse, eye-sized, dark spots; belly yellowish-white.
Habitat In rivers and large lakes in Yugoslavia and Albania. Lives in rivers that emerge from beneath the limestone hills in relatively cool, but clean water.
Food A general predator on small crustaceans, insect larvae, and for larger specimens, small fishes.
Breeding Not known. Probably shares the general habit of trout by spawning in gravel beds in early winter.
Range Occurs only in the rivers of Yugoslavia and Albania and in Lake Ohrid. A vulnerable species, the isolated populations in these rivers are small, and the rivers are threatened by water abstraction, dams for hydro-electric use. In addition, introductions of brown trout from fish farms threaten this rare native species.

Huchen
Hucho hucho

Family name Salmonidae (salmons and trouts)
Length 1.5m (4ft 11in); formerly much larger
Weight about 18kg (40lb)

Identification Salmon-like in body form but with a deep caudal peduncle, side of body flattened. Adipose fin present; head pointed and long; upper jawbone reaches beyond rear of the eye. Scales very small. Coloration green or greeny-blue, sides silvery with a pink sheen, white below. The back has small x-shaped dark spots. Spawning fish are coppery-red in colour.
Habitat Lives in large rivers in swiftly flowing parts as well as backwaters. The young fish live in shallow water close to rocks, often in tributaries.
Food The young eat crustaceans and small fishes; the adults eat large fishes, amphibians and occasionally aquatic mammals.
Breeding Spawns in early spring on gravel banks in a redd made by the female. Eggs are buried in the gravel but hatch in about 5 weeks.
Range Native to the Danube, but now much restricted in its range owing to developments and pollution locally. Has been introduced to France, and the UK unsuccessfully. Huchen is a protected species in several E. European countries, and is also raised in hatcheries to supplement the native stock.

Arctic Charr
Salvelinus alpinus

Family name Salmonidae (salmons and trouts)
Length 30cm (12in) in lakes; migratory forms 1.0m (3ft 3in)
Weight up to 3.58kg (7lb 14oz)

Identification Trout-like in general form with an adipose fin,
but with very small scales. The upper jawbone reaches just
past the rear edge of the eye. Sea-run charr (found only at the
N. edge of their range) are silvery with reddish or pink spots
on sides, the belly is orange to red; Lake charr are greeny-
brown with reddish and white spots on the sides, the belly is
orange to red. Both forms have white edges to the pectoral,
pelvic and anal fins.
Habitat Exists in two forms. In central and N. Europe in
deep mountain lakes where it lives between the lake bed and
mid-water. In northernmost parts of north Europe migratory,
living in rivers and migrating to the sea in winter.
Food In lakes and as young in rivers eats mainly planktonic
crustaceans; larger specimens eat small fishes. The migratory
form eats crustaceans and fishes in the sea.
Breeding Spawning takes place in winter or early spring. The
lake charr migrate into feeder streams or spawn on gravel beds
at the edge of the lake. Migratory fish breed in gravel in river
beds. Both shed their eggs in redds cut by the female in the
gravel.
Range Migratory forms close to the Arctic Circle in rivers and
the sea. Land-locked populations in Scandinavia, northern
UK, Ireland and the Alpine lakes (including N. Italy and
Austria).

Brook Charr
Salvelinus fontinalis

Family name Salmonidae (salmons and trouts)
Length 45cm (17¾in); migratory forms in N. America
are larger
Weight up to 4.5kg (10lb)

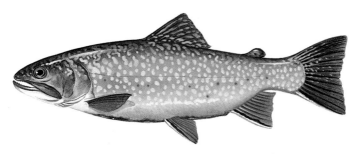

Identification Trout-like in general form with an adipose fin
and very small scales. The upper jawbone is very long and
reaches well beyond the rear of the eye. Olive green to brown
on the back, sides lighter; the sides have creamy spots running
together into wavy lines on the back. Dorsal and tail fins have
wavy cream lines. The front edges of the pectoral, pelvic and
anal fins are white with a dark band behind the white.
Habitat Lives in cool, well-oxygenated streams and lakes. In
the north of its range migrates to the sea.
Food Mainly insects, insect larvae, crustaceans and small
fishes (large specimens). In the sea mostly crustaceans and
fishes. Takes insects and arthropods fallen from overhanging
trees.
Breeding Spawns in late summer to autumn in gravel beds in
shallow streams near the head of the river. Lake populations
may spawn in gravel near the lake shore but usually migrate
into inflowing streams.
Range Native to eastern North America (N. Canada to Cape
Cod and westwards to the Great Lakes). Has been introduced
to many lakes in Europe.

Vendace
Coregonus albula

Family name Salmonidae (salmons and trouts);
sometimes Coregonidae
Length 35cm (14in); usually much smaller
Weight about .45kg (1lb)

Identification Flat-sided, silvery fish with an adipose fin and
relatively large scales. The lower jaw is curved upwards and
the mouth opens on the upper side of the head. Gill rakers on
the first gill arch numerous, 36–52 in number. Coloration,
back greeny-blue, sides and belly silvery; fins on the upper side
dusky; tip of the snout dark.
Habitat In lakes in mountainous regions in N. Europe; in the
N. of its range in rivers migrating to estuaries (as in the Baltic)
or lakes in winter.
Food In lakes feeds almost exclusively on planktonic
crustaceans. In rivers and some large lakes eats molluscs,
insect larvae, and crustaceans.
Breeding Spawns in early winter in shallow water in lakes,
the eggs being shed over gravel beds. River-dwelling stocks
migrate upstream to spawn.
Range Isolated lakes in the UK (Bassenthwaite and
Derwentwater in English Lake District, formerly in Castle and
Mill Lochs, Loch Mabern, Scotland) and in the Alpine lakes,
Scandinavian countries and western USSR. Generally a
vulnerable species.

Schelly
Coregonus laveretus

Family name Salmonidae (salmons and trouts), sometimes Coregonidae
Length 30cm (12in); occasionally larger
Weight up to 0.95kg (2lb 1oz)

Identification A robust whitefish, with a relatively deep body and smoothly curved back, the sides flat. An adipose fin is present and the scales are large. The mouth is ventral, with the upper jaw overhanging. (In the migratory, estuarine form, known as the houting, the snout is protuberant.) Back blue or blue-green, sides silvery; fins greyish, at least at their tips.
Habitat In isolated mountain lakes in UK – Llyn Tegid (Gwyniad), Ullswater, Haweswater (Schelly), Loch Lomond and Lake Eck (Powan) – also N. Europe and to the N. in estuarine conditions and rivers.
Food Mostly planktonic crustaceans, bottom-living insect larvae and crustaceans in estuarines.
Breeding Spawns in winter on gravel beds in lakes and in deep parts of rivers following an upstream migration. The eggs lie buried in the gravel and hatch in early spring.
Range Lakes in the UK (see above), Alpine lakes, and around the Baltic basin, entering that sea. Formerly found in the eastern North Sea, along the Dutch and German coasts (now extinct there).

Pollan
Coregonus autumnalis

Family name Salmonidae (salmons and trouts);
sometimes Coregonidae
Length 25cm (9¾in); occasionally larger
Weight up to 1kg (2.2lb)

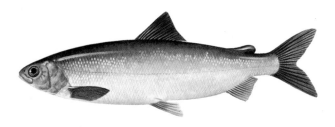

Identification A robust whitefish, with a relatively deep body
and smoothly curved back from the snout tip to the dorsal fin.
Adipose fin present; scales large. The mouth is at the tip of the
snout, the jaws only slightly angled; neither jaw projects.
Coloration silvery, bluish on the back; the fins dusky.

Habitat In Europe lives only in Loughs Neagh and Erne in
Northern Ireland. Widely distributed in these large lakes.
Food Eats the shrimp-like crustacean *Mysis relicta*, also
bottom-living insect larvae, crustaceans, small molluscs and fry
of fishes.
Breeding Spawns on the lake bed in November and
December over rocky or gravel beds.
Range In Europe only in the two Irish loughs (see above);
elsewhere in north-western N. America (Alaska and the N.W.
Territories). May also occur in Arctic USSR.

Grayling
Thymallus thymallus

Family name Thymallidae (graylings)
Length 50cm (20in); exceptionally larger
Weight up to 2.5kg (5lb 8oz)

Identification Adipose fin present. Body flat-sided and moderately deep, but with a small head and pointed snout. Dorsal fin high (especially in males) and many-rayed (17–24 rays). Scales moderately large. Coloration on the back steel-blue to greeny-brown, sides silvery but with faint violet stripes. Dorsal fin with rows of dusky spots.
Habitat Lives in clean, cool, well-oxygenated rivers, also occurs in some natural lakes, often in mountainous regions.
Food Bottom-living insect larvae, crustaceans and even molluscs. Also eats insects and other small animals that drop into the water from bank-side vegetation.
Breeding Spawns in spring on gravelly shallows in a shallow redd made by the female. The coloration of the male is brighter at spawning time and there is some display; the male's dorsal fin is wrapped over the female's back.
Range From England and Wales across Europe to the Black Sea, and from N. Sweden southwards to France and the Alps. Often introduced to rivers by angling interests.

Smelt
Osmerus eperlanus

Family name Osmeridae (smelts)
Length maximum 30cm (12in); mostly much smaller

Identification Similar to the salmon and trout in general form but much smaller. An adipose fin present. Jaws long and with strong teeth. Smells strongly of cucumber. Back light olive-brown, the belly creamy white; an indistinct silvery line on the sides.
Habitat Inshore migratory fish which spawns in fresh water or where the salinity is very low. It is caught most commonly in upper estuaries. A few populations live in fresh water coastal lakes.
Food Planktonic crustaceans and small fishes.
Breeding Enters rivers in winter and early spring, the eggs are laid on gravel beds, over sandbanks, or amongst plants in spring. The eggs stick to the gravel and plants but often break away in the river's flow and then float in the water, buoyed up by the outer egg membrane. The young fish move downstream in autumn.
Range From the west coast of Ireland and the N. Irish Sea eastwards. Abundant in parts of the North Sea and the Baltic. In a few freshwater lakes in S. Sweden and the Baltic states; formerly in Rostherne Mere (Cheshire) in UK. Has been affected by pollution in estuaries and lower rivers and in places is now scarce.

Eel
Anguilla anguilla

Family name Anguillidae
Length 50cm (20in) (M); 1.0m (3ft 3in) (F)
Weight up to 5kg (11lb) (F)

Identification Distinctive eel shape but with origin of dorsal fin about third of the way down the body. Pectoral fin rounded. Lower jaw is longer than the upper, and protrudes beyond it; eye small; a small gill slit in front of pectoral fin. Coloration variable, usually brownish on back, yellowish on sides. In maturing ('silver') eels the back becomes black and the belly silvery; the eye also increases in size.
Habitat In fresh water in lakes and rivers, usually buried in the mud or lying close to the banks or in tree roots, emerging in the half-light. Many eels live in the lower estuaries of rivers and in coastal waters on the shore. Young stages (elvers) are seen in estuaries migrating upstream; the post-larvae (leptocephali) live in the open ocean.
Food Eat bottom-living invertebrates (crustaceans, worms, molluscs and insect larvae), dead fish and other carrion.
Breeding Migrates to mid-Atlantic to spawn. The post-larvae migrate across the Atlantic taking about 3 years to reach the Atlantic coast and 4 years to reach the eastern Mediterranean. They arrive in the UK in spring as glass eels, then turn to elvers.
Range Coastal Europe from Iceland and mid-Norway, S. to Morocco and throughout the Mediterranean. Most unpolluted rivers in this area will contain eels.

Pike
Esox lucius

Family name Esocidae (pikes)
Length 1.30m (4ft 3in) (F)
Weight 24kg (53lb)

Identification Long, torpedo-shaped body with dorsal and anal fins close to the tail fin. Head pointed from side view; snout flat. The lower jaws with several massive fangs; hundreds of small sharp teeth on palate. Coloration, greenish-brown above, the sides greenish, flecked with gold lines and speckles on sides, sometimes forming bars. The colour pattern is specific to the individual.
Habitat Lakes and slow-flowing rivers or canals. Young fish often lie close to the surface amongst plants; adults lurk in deep water under cover; typically lie hidden in vegetation.
Food Juveniles eat invertebrates, young fish, tadpoles, etc.; adults eat fishes, frogs, water voles, and the largest will eat ducklings and other water birds occasionally.
Breeding Spawns in early spring in flooded water-meadow ditches or at the edge of flooded rivers. Often 2–3 males accompany the much larger female. The eggs are shed over water plants. Mature in 2–3 years.
Range Northern Europe from Ireland and N. Scandinavia eastwards through the USSR, Siberia, and across northern North America (where known as northern pike).

Mudminnow

Umbra krameri

Family name Umbridae (mudminnows)
Length 13cm (5in) (F); males are smaller

Identification A small, rather stout fish with scales extending over head and body. Dorsal fin about twice length of base of anal fin; both set near the tail fin. Coloration, greenish-brown on the back with dusky vertical bars on the sides; yellowish on the belly.

Habitat Lives in swamps, overgrown ponds and oxbows, in depths of 0.5–6.0m (1ft 6in–19ft 7in) in regions where the bottom contains deep, black silt from decaying vegetation. Such habitats are often deoxygenated in the summer and under snow in winter, and the only other fish to live in them are crucian carp and pond loach.

Food Small insect larvae, particularly midge larvae (bloodworms), crustaceans and molluscs. Young mudminnows feed on small crustaceans, e.g. water fleas and ostracods.

Breeding In spring, about 150 eggs being laid by the female in a shallow hollow made among plant roots. The young attach themselves to aquatic plants after hatching.

Range In the backwaters and flood plains of the Danube basin, in Austria, Hungary, Romania and Czechoslovakia. In many places becoming rare as river flows are controlled and flood plains drained. Nearest relative is the eastern mudminnow, *U. pygmaea*, from eastern North America, introduced to Holland and parts of France.

Carp
Cyprinus carpio

Family name Cyprinidae (carps and minnows)
Length 1.5m (4ft 11in)
Weight 36kg (80lb); usually less

Identification Scaleless head and usually fully scaled body (except in mirror carp and leather carp varieties). Dorsal fin long based, free edge concave; a stout spine (with serrated rear edges as first ray). Mouth toothless but with 2 barbels each side, second one longer. Coloration variable; wild fish usually greenish-brown on back, yellowish on belly. Forms hybrids with crucian carp. Koi carp are multicoloured variety of this species, kept as ornamental fish.
Habitat Large lakes and major rivers in slow-flowing lowland areas. The native carp of eastern and central Europe are slender bodied compared with fat, artificially reared specimens.
Food Vegetation and bottom-living insect larvae, snails, crustaceans and worms.
Breeding Late spring in shallow, sun-warmed areas over dense vegetation. The eggs and newly hatched young are attached to the plants.
Range Natural range, the Danube basin eastwards to Siberia and China, including the larger lowland lakes of eastern Europe. Because it is popular as a food and angling fish has been widely introduced in western Europe, especially warmer areas, and elsewhere in the world. Many of these introductions have been via fish farms and involve heavy-bodied, fast-growing fish.

Crucian Carp
Carassius carassius

Family name Cyprinidae (carps and minnows)
Length 51cm (20in); often much smaller
Weight 1.8kg (4lb)

Identification Scaleless head and fully scaled body. Dorsal fin long based, the free edge convex; a lightly serrated spine at the front of the fin, 14–21 branched rays. No barbels around mouth. Body deep in large specimens. Coloration, olive-green with bronze tint on the sides. Ventral fins have reddish tinge; others are dark greeny-brown. Forms hybrids with carp and goldfish.
Habitat Lives in marshy pools, overgrown lakes and backwaters of rivers. Tolerates high and very low temperatures as well as low oxygen levels and can survive in shallow, stagnant water where few other fish could live. Usually associated with heavy plant growth.
Food Mostly plants, also eats insect larvae, crustaceans and molluscs. Young feed on planktonic crustaceans.
Breeding Spawns in May and June. The golden eggs are stuck to plants. Young fish hatch out in 5–7 days but stay on plants for several further days. Some populations survive from all-female stock.
Range Eastern England eastwards to central USSR. Widely introduced elsewhere. Pure-bred crucian carp have become uncommon in many parts of their native range as a result of interbreeding with goldfish.

Goldfish
Carassius auratus

Family name Cyprinidae (carps and minnows)
Length 30.5cm (12in)
Weight 0.9g (2lb); usually much smaller

Identification Exists as two forms: the eastern European gibel carp, greeny-brown on back and sides, whitish ventrally; Asiatic form, greenish when young usually changing to golden-red as adult. Body shape very variable. Head scaleless, no barbels around mouth. Dorsal fin long based, concave free edge. Anal fin with 5–6 branched rays. Both fins with strongly serrated spine in front.
Habitat Mostly found in lowland rivers, lakes and ponds as a result of introduction. Gibel carp, native to estern Europe, lives in densely weeded small lakes and ponds.
Food Feeds on plants, insect larvae, crustaceans and molluscs.
Breeding Eggs are laid on water plants in June to July. They hatch in 7–9 days; young fish stay attached to plants. Both goldfish and gibel carp hybridize with crucian carp to produce fertile offspring. In many areas of eastern Europe they have ousted the crucian carp, and form populations of complex hybrid form. Some gibel carp populations are female only, the eggs developing as a result of stimulation (but not fertilization) by sperm of other species.
Range Originally from central Europe east to China and Korea, now totally confused as a result of introductions.

Bitterling
Rhodeus sericeus

Family name Cyprinidae (carps and minnows)
Length 7cm (2¾in); exceptionally to 9cm (3½in)

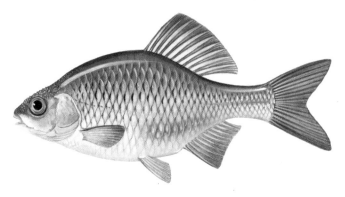

Identification Deep-bodied with large scales on body.
Lateral line confined to 5 or 6 scales behind head. Dorsal fin
relatively high and with 8–9 branched rays. Head small; eye
comparatively large. Coloration varies with season; back is
mostly olive green, sides silvery with a pinkish flush; silvery on
the belly. A bright metallic stripe along the sides near the tail.
In spawning season this becomes brilliantly iridescent in
males.
Habitat Lives in small ponds, lakes and overgrown lowland
rivers in which the water flows very slowly. Amongst plants in
clear water; in turbid areas will be found in open water.
Food Planktonic crustaceans; aquatic insect larvae both in
vegetation and on bed of pond, especially midge larvae.
Breeding Unique among European fishes as eggs are laid in
mantle-cavity of freshwater mussel. Male adopts territory
around mussel. Female developes a long filament from the
genital opening which is used to stimulate mussel to open the
valves of its shell; the eggs are then shed in to the gill chamber
of the mollusc and the male's sperm is ejected near the
inhalant siphon so that the eggs are fertilized inside the mussel.
Relatively few, but large (*c* 3mm) eggs are produced. They
hatch in 21–27 days.
Range Originally central Europe and Danube basin, but
introduced to much of W. Europe, including England, where
it is now widespread.

False Rasbora
Pseudorasbora parva

Family name Cyprinidae (carps and minnows)
Length 6cm (2½in)

Identification A small, slender fish with the body slightly compressed from side to side. Body fully scaled; the lateral line straight, running from head to tail. The head is pointed and compressed; no barbels around the mouth. The mouth is oblique but opens at the tip of the snout. Coloration, olive brown above, the scales with dark crescent-shaped speckles (adults speckled all over, including the fins). Narrow dark line running from head to tail fin along the sides. Fins almost black at breeding time.
Habitat Slow-flowing rivers and lakes. An active fish which swims in mid-water in small schools.
Food Planktonic crustaceans and young fishes; possibly also fish eggs. It is believed to feed heavily on the fry of some fishes and to have adversely affected the population. This may, however, be true only in the few years after it has become established.
Breeding Not known.
Range Native to eastern Asia from the Amur basin, China, Korea, Taiwan and parts of Japan. Introduced to the Danube accidently with Chinese carp in 1960, it has spread widely into Romania, Hungary, Czechoslovakia, Austria and Germany. It has now been found in Yugoslavia, Albania, parts of Greece; spread in some areas as food for predatory fish.

Grass Carp
Ctenopharyngodon idella

Family name Cyprinidae (carps and minnows)
Length 1.25m (4ft 1¼in)
Weight approx. 35g (77lb)

Identification Slender-bodied with a large, very broad head and wide mouth; eyes small and placed on sides of head. Head scaleless; body scales moderately large (43–45 in lateral line). Dorsal and anal fins short based, rounded in outline. Coloration, dark greeny-brown back, but with dusky centre to scales; sides pale golden.
Habitat Native to R. Amur and eastern Asia and normally an inhabitant of large rivers and oxbow lakes in their flood plains. Introduced to western Europe (including UK) in reservoirs, large lakes and some large rivers.
Food Juveniles and adults eat plant matter and, depending on size of stock, will virtually clear choked waters of plants, even eating the bankside vegetation. Young fish also eat aquatic insect larvae and crustaceans.
Breeding In native habitat breeds in early spring during the seasonal flooding of the rivers. All European fish are raised on fish farms.
Range R. Amur and E. Asia. Introduced to Europe for its ability to control dense aquatic vegetation, and in places for its size-appeal to anglers; also inland for food.

Silver Carp
Hypophthalmichthys molitrix

Family name Cyprinidae (carps and minnows)
Length 1.0m (3ft 3in)
Weight 8kg (17lb 9 oz)

Identification Rather deep-bodied. Head relatively small with the mouth strongly oblique and opening on the upper surface. Eyes set very low, at level of mouth or below. Body covered with small scales, 110–125 in lateral line, which runs in a downward curve parallel to the belly. Dorsal fin short based; anal fin long based, strongly concave. Coloration silvery, dusky on the back; fins dark.
Habitat Native to the R. Amur where it lives in deep pools and in flood plain lakes. Survives well in reservoirs, impounded lakes, and still waters generally.
Food Feeds on plankton, mainly the minute, floating plant plankton in the surface waters. Adapted to this diet by its fine, long gill rakers on the gill arches which act as a filter to catch the phytoplankton.
Breeding In the R. Amur breeds in early summer in backwaters and lakes close to the lake outlet to the river. Does not breed in the wild in Europe; stock are raised in fish farms and then released.
Range Native to the Amur basin in Siberia. Introduced to many large reservoirs and other still waters, particularly in eastern Europe. Important commercially in inland areas; attractive as a cultivated fish as it uses plant plankton directly as food.

Roach
Rutilus rutilus

Family name Cyprinidae (carps and minnows)
Length maximum 53cm (21in); usually up to 35cm (13¾in)
Weight 1.8kg (4lb)

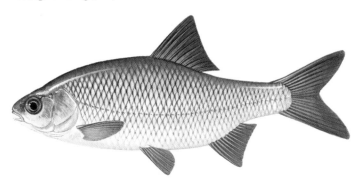

Identification Moderately deep-bodied with a small head; young fish are more slender. Head scaleless, body with large scales; 42–45 scales in the lateral line. Dorsal and anal fins both short based; anal fin with 9–11 branched rays. The dorsal fin lies vertically above the base of the pelvic fins. Coloration distinctive; iris of the eye red; pelvic and anal fins orange to bright red, pectoral fins reddish. Dorsal and tail fins dusky. Back blue-greeny brown; sides intensely silver.
Habitat Lowland lakes and rivers, especially slow-flowing rivers. Particularly common where there is good weed growth. Because it is popular with anglers is often introduced to marginally suitable habitats.
Food Eats aquatic insect larvae, insects, crustaceans, snails and a lot of plant matter. Juveniles eat small crustaceans such as water fleas.
Breeding Spawns April–June, shedding its yellowish eggs over plants, algae and even tree roots where plants are scarce. The eggs stick to the vegetation and hatch in 9–12 days.
Range Native to eastern England and from France and Sweden eastwards to the Urals. Widely introduced and now occurs in Ireland, Wales and Scotland.

Danubian Roach

Rutilus pigus

Family name Cyprinidae (carps and minnows)
Length 40cm (15¾in); usually a good deal smaller

Identification Moderately deep-bodied but with a small head. Head scaleless; body fully scaled with 45–49 scales in the lateral line. Dorsal and anal fins short based; the anal fin has 10–13 branched rays; dorsal fin 10–11 branched rays. This eastern European species is similar to the roach but has slightly smaller, more numerous scales. Coloration, olive-brown on the back, sides brassy-yellow, silvery ventrally. Anal and pelvic fins are reddish.
Habitat Slow-flowing rivers and lakes with abundant vegetation. Is less common in rivers where the current is moderate.
Food Feeds on larval stages of aquatic insects, other small invertebrates, water plants and algae.
Breeding Spawns in late spring. Eggs are adhesive and fixed to water plants. Forms large schools when spawning.
Range Apparently represented by two subspecies. *Rutilus pigus pigus* occurs in N. Italy (the Po basin) and *R. p. virgo* is found in the middle reaches of the Danube. The Danube population is said to have declined in size but there is little information about the numbers of either form.

Italian Roach
Rutilus rubilio

Family name Cyprinidae (carps and minnows)
Length grows to 20cm (8in)

Identification Moderately deep-bodied with a small head and a rounded snout. Head scaleless; body with moderately large scales, 36–44 in the lateral line. Both dorsal and anal fins are short based but the dorsal fin is high. Branched rays in dorsal 8–9; branched rays in anal 8–10. Coloration, olive-brown on the back, silver-white on the sides and belly. The sides have a poorly defined grey to black stripe along them.
Habitat Lives in still waters and rivers with slow current; always in areas where the aquatic plants are dense and always seen in large schools.
Food A generalist feeder, eating aquatic insects and their larvae, crustaceans, and plant food. In some warm-water springs seems to feed on filamentous algae only.
Breeding Spawns in late spring, end of March to June. The eggs are small and yellowish and are scattered on plant leaves and algae.
Range Most abundant in Italy and found all over that country (except for Sardinia and Sicily). Probably widely redistributed by man. It is also found along the Adriatic rivers of Yugoslavia, Albania and Greece. Elsewhere in Greece similar forms occur which may be different species.

Escalo
Rutilus arcasii

Family name Cyprinidae (carps and minnows)
Length maximum 13cm (5in)

Identification A small, roach-like species with a slender body
and a small head. As is typical of the family, the head is
scaleless, while the body is fully covered with scales, with
40–46 in the lateral line. The profile of the head is gently
curved, although it is steep on the snout; the eyes are large, in
diameter about equal to the snout. Dorsal fin very short based;
originating above the base of the pelvic fins; the anal fin has a
shorter base than the dorsal. Coloration, the back is medium
brown, the sides silvery fading to white on the belly. A silvery-
grey line runs along the side; it is composed of fine, dark
pigment cells. The fin rays on the ventral fins are reddish but
the membranes are clear.
Habitat Lives in schools in streams in upland areas and also
in slow-flowing rivers.
Food Eats insect larvae and crustaceans; some flying insects
are taken at the surface.
Breeding Not known; believed to spawn in the spring.
Distribution Found in Portugal and parts of western Spain;
does not extend to the southern rivers.

Rudd
Scardinus erythrophthalmus

Family name Cyprinidae (carps and minnows)
Length up to 45cm (17¾in)
Weight up to 2kg (4lb 6oz)

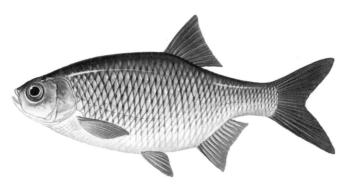

Identification Deep-bodied with a rather small head. Head
scaleless, the mouth steeply angled to open on the upper edge
of the snout. Dorsal fin short based, rather high, its origin
vertically behind the level of the base of the pelvic fins. Anal
fin with 10–11 branched rays. The scales across the belly
(between the pelvic and anal fins) form a sharp keel.
Coloration, deep greeny-brown on the back, sides bronze-
yellow, ventrally creamy. All the fins are reddish, the pelvic
and anal fins a brilliant blood red. Iris of eye golden with a red
fleck above it.
Habitat Lives in oxbows and backwaters of large lowland
rivers, also in lakes. Has been widely introduced to less typical
waters. Thrives in heavily weeded waters and survives in areas
where dissolved oxygen is low.
Food Young rudd feed on insect larvae, crustaceans and
algae; large specimens feed heavily on plant matter but also eat
aquatic insects. Feed near the surface of the water and often
take surface-living insects.
Breeding Spawns April to June amongst dense vegetation
and at the edges of reed beds. The eggs stick to the plants and
hatch in 8–15 days.
Range Widely distributed across Europe from England to the
Urals and southern Sweden to northern Italy and Greece.
Introduced to many regions, including Wales and Ireland.

Greek Rudd
Scardinius graecus

Family name Cyprinidae (carps and minnows)
Length maximum 40cm (15¾in); usually to about 25cm
(9¾in)

Identification A slender-bodied 'rudd' with a relatively large
head which is also shallow. Head scaleless; body fully scaled
with large scales forming a distinct keel between the pelvic and
anal fins. Head and snout strongly concave in profile with a
large, steeply angled mouth. Dorsal fin short based and rather
high, its origin behind the pelvic fin base; anal fin also short
based. Coloration, greenish-brown on the back and upper
sides, fading to yellowish, thence to bright silvery on the sides.
Pectoral, pelvic and anal fins slightly red-tinged but otherwise
grey; the remaining fins dark grey. (The main distinguishing
features of this species are the number of vertebrae and its
geographical range.)
Habitat Lives in two lakes in Greece and is usually found in
open water close to weed beds.
Breeding Said to spawn amongst weeds in shallow water
from April to June.
Food A plant eater. The young eat planktonic algae and
diatoms; adults eat higher plants in large quantities.
Range Found only in Lakes Yliki and Paralimni (Beotia) in
the extreme east of mainland Greece. It does not occur
elsewhere in Greece.

Acheloos Rudd
Scardinius acarnanicus

Family name Cyprinidae (carps and minnows)
Length maximum 30cm (12in)

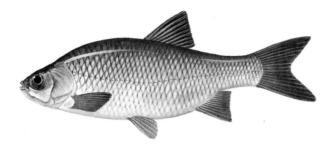

Identification A rather slender-bodied 'rudd' with an apparently large head. Head scaleless, strongly concave snout and 'forehead'. The mouth very steeply angled to open on the upper edge of the snout. Dorsal fin short based, moderate in height, its origin well behind the origin of the pelvic fins. Anal fin short based with 10–11 branched rays. Body scales rather large, forming a keel between the pelvic and anal fins. Coloration, sides brilliantly silvery, back olive-brown, eye yellowish; the pectoral, pelvic and anal fins dark grey with only a slight tinge of red; other fins dark. (The main distinguishing features of this species are the number of vertebrae and its geographical range.)
Habitat Lives in lakes and the slow-flowing reaches of rivers. Generally found in close proximity to beds of aquatic vegetation in 1–20m (3–66ft) of water.
Breeding Not recorded.
Feeding This species has recently been shown to be almost wholly a herbivore. The young fish eat plant plankton; adults eat a wide range of higher plants, even marsh plants when the lakes are flooded seasonally.
Range Found only in the Acheloos river system of western Greece, particularly in Lake Trichonis and Lake Lyssimachia where it is commercially fished.

Bream
Abramis brama

Family name Cyprinidae (carps and minnows)
Length exceptionally to 80cm (31½in)
Weight exceptionally to 9kg (19lb 10oz)

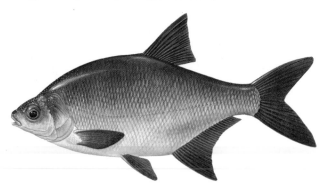

Identification Very deep-bodied with flat sides and high back; young specimens are more slender. Head scaleless, relatively small, the eyes small and the mouth can extend ventrally to form a tube. Body scales small; 51–60 in the lateral line. Anal fin long based with 24–30 branched rays; its outline strongly concave. Coloration, dark brown or greyish on back, sides golden-brown; young bream are silvery sided. Fins greyish-brown, ventrally tinted with red.
Habitat Lives in deep, slow-flowing rivers, backwaters and in flood-plain lakes, reservoirs and flooded gravel pits. It lives close to the bottom in schools. At night moves into shallow water to feed.
Food Strongly dependent on bottom-living insect larvae, worms, molluscs and crustaceans. The down-turned tubular mouth is ideal for sucking such organisms from the lake bed.
Breeding Spawns in late spring and early summer amongst dense plant growth, mostly at night, and in shallow water. Yellowish eggs stick to the weeds.
Range From Ireland eastwards to the Urals and from the northern Baltic to the Pyrenees and Alps in the south; throughout the Danube basin. Introduced to Ireland, Scotland and parts of Europe for angling and commercial fisheries.

Zope
Abramis ballerus

Family name Cyprinidae (carps and minnows)
Length maximum 41cm (16in); usually 30–36cm (12–14in)

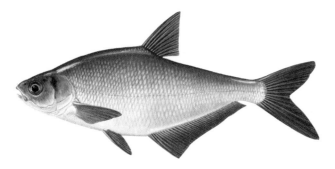

Identification Body flattened from side to side but not particularly deep. Head scaleless, rather small; the eyes are moderate in size, their diameter about equal to the snout length. Mouth angled, opening just on the upper edge of the snout. Body scales small 66–73 in lateral line. Dorsal fin short based and high; anal fin very long based, 36–43 branched rays. Coloration, dark greeny-blue on back, the sides silvery with a golden sheen on the upper flanks. Fins are greyish but pectorals and pelvics are yellowish with dusky edges.
Habitat Lives in slow-flowing rivers and lakes in their flood plains. Adults live in open water but gather close to the bottom in cold weather; the young live in reed beds in shallower water.
Food Feeds mainly on animal plankton (chiefly crustaceans), but will also eat insect larvae from among water plants.
Breeding Becomes mature in 3–4 years. Migrates up river or into shallow parts of lakes to spawn close to weed beds and gravel-bottomed areas. Spawns in April and May.
Range In the Danube and Volga river basins, particularly in their upper reaches. Also in rivers running into the Baltic, including some Swedish rivers, but in this area is very sparse.

Danubian Bream
Abramis sapa

Family name Cyprinidae (carps and minnows)
Length maximum about 30cm (12in); usually 15–20cm (6–8in)
Weight 0.8kg (1lb 12oz)

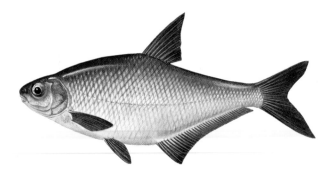

Identification Similar in body shape to the Zope with a flattened body and moderately high back. The head is small, but the eyes are relatively large (diameter larger than snout length); the snout is blunt and the mouth terminal. Body scales relatively large; 48–52 in lateral line. Dorsal fin narrow based and high; anal fin very long based, 36–41 branched rays. Coloration dusky green on the back, silvery on the sides. All the fins are dusky.
Habitat A bottom-living schooling fish found in the lower reaches of rivers and in estuarine conditions near the river mouth.
Food Almost entirely bottom-living invertebrates, midge larvae, amphipods, molluscs; the young feed on ostracods.
Breeding Breeds in its fourth year or later, in April to May. Spawns in the main stream of the river over dense vegetation and close to clean gravel. The populations living in brackish conditions migrate upstream into fresh water to spawn.
Range The Danube basin and rivers flowing into the Black, Caspian and Aral Seas. Has become less common in the Danube, probably as a result of river impoundments and poor water quality. Its status elsewhere is little known.

Zährte

Vimba vimba

Family name Cyprinidae (carps and minnows)
Length maximum about 50cm (20in); usually between
20–40cm (8–16in)
Weight about 0.9kg (2lb)

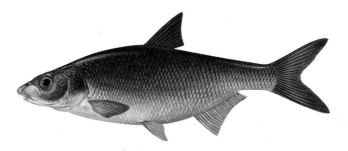

Identification Compared with the breams this is a slender-bodied fish with only moderately compressed sides. The head is small; the snout fleshy and projecting and the mouth is entirely ventral. Dorsal fin short based; anal fin long based with 18–21 branched rays. Body scales small, 57–63 in lateral line. A scaleless keel between the anal and tail fins, and a keel covered with scales behind the dorsal fin. Coloration blue-grey on the back; yellowish-silver on the sides and belly. At spawning the back becomes very dark and the belly orange-red.
Habitat Lives in the middle reaches of rivers in eastern Europe but also occurring close to the mouths of these rivers. Lives close to the river bed.
Food Feeds on the bottom on molluscs, worms and crustaceans.
Breeding Spawns in May to July in shallow water on the river bed over gravel where it is clear of mud and silt. Spawning follows an upstream migration often over long distances.
Range Occurs in the rivers of the Baltic Sea but has become very rare in Sweden and in German and Polish rivers. Also lives in the rivers feeding the Black and Caspian Seas. Best known in the Danube system.

Silver bream
Blicca bjoerkna

Family name Cyprinidae (carps and minnows)
Length maximum 36cm (14in); usually up to 25cm (9¾in)
Weight 0.45g (1lb)

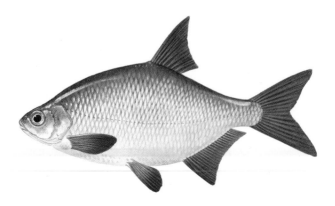

Identification Moderately deep bodied with a high back and flattened from side to side. The head is small, scaleless, and the eye is moderately large (equal to the length of the snout). Dorsal fin short based and high; anal fin long based with 21–23 branched rays. Body scales moderately large, 44–48 in the lateral line. Coloration, light olive-brown on the back, sides brilliant silver. Fins are dusky except for the pectoral and pelvic fins which are orange with grey tips.

Habitat Most abundant in large, slow-flowing lowland rivers and their flood plains; often found in reservoirs and flooded gravel pits and may be common in these man-made waters.

Food Feeds in both mid-water on planktonic crustaceans, and on insect larvae on vegetation, and also on the bottom on a variety of invertebrates.

Breeding Spawns amongst plants in summer in small schools. The yellow-coloured eggs stick to the plant leaves.

Range Distributed widely in Europe, from the rivers of eastern England and northern France eastwards to the Caspian Sea. From southern Sweden and the Baltic states southwards to the Alps, it is particularly common in the Danube basin.

Bleak
Alburnus alburnus

Family name Cyprinidae (carps and minnows)
Length maximum 20cm (8in); usually only up to 15cm (6in)

Identification Slim bodied and slender. Head scaleless, pointed, with an oblique mouth opening on the upper surface of the head. Eyes relatively large. Scales relatively large, very thin and fragile; easily dislodged; 48–55 in the lateral line. Anal fin long based, concave at edge, with 16–20 branched rays. Coloration, back and upper sides blue-green, lower sides and belly brilliant silver. The fins are greyish; white ventrally.
Habitat Lives mainly in slow-flowing lowland rivers but penetrates well upstream to the middle reaches of rivers. Survives well in turbid and poorly oxygenated water but is then seen mostly at the surface.
Food Eats animal plankton, especially small crustaceans, flying insects when they settle on the water and aerial insects. It is particularly well equipped to feed at the surface.
Breeding Spawns in May or June in shallow water over stones or shallow weed beds.
Range Occurs from E. England eastwards to the Ural Mountains, and from S. Sweden to S. France and N.E. Greece. Has been introduced to the western rivers of England.

Alborella
Alburnus albidus

Family name Cyprinidae (carps and minnows)
Length maximum 20cm (8in); usually less

Identification Very similar to the bleak. Slender-bodied with a small, scaleless head, rather large eyes and strongly upturned mouth which opens just on the upper side of the snout. The dorsal fin origin is just to the posterior of the pelvics. Anal fin rather long based, 13–17 branched rays. Scales rather large, fragile, 42–51 in the lateral line. Coloration, grey-green above with a side line of green edged with gold.
Habitat A schooling fish which lives in streams and rivers and also in the Alpine lakes of N. Italy. It lives both near the surface and in mid-water.
Food Eats mostly planktonic animals, particularly crustaceans, small aquatic insects and insect larvae. Particularly well adapted to take food at the surface. Also reported to eat some algae.
Breeding Breeds in summer, June to August, over gravel beds and near weed banks.
Range Confined to N. Italy and the Adriatic rivers of the Balkans. Another, separate population is found at the S. end of Italy. Numerous subspecies have been described but their relationships are poorly known.

Schneider

Alburnoides bipunctatus

Family name Cyprinidae (carps and minnows)
Length maximum 15cm (6in); usually less

Identification A small, rather slender fish with a small, scaleless head. The eyes are moderately large, and the mouth is rather large, opening at the tip of the snout and continuing back to the eye level. Scales rather small, lateral line strongly curved downwards with 44–52 scales. Anal fin long based, with a concave free edge; 14–17 branched rays. Coloration, light olive-green on the back, silvery below; a diffuse yellowish line along the sides, the lateral line with dark points along its length.
Habitat Most common in small rivers and medium-sized streams, less so in the main river. It prefers clean, running water over stony or rocky bottoms, even riffles. Frequently found with minnows and trout.
Food Eats insect larvae mostly and crustaceans but a substantial part of its food are insects which fall into the water from bankside trees and plants.
Breeding The eggs are laid on sand or gravel in swiftly flowing water in May to June. The eggs drop among the stones and adhere to them.
Range From central France to the Volga and along the S.E. border of the Black Sea southwards to Greece. Numerous subspecies described from Turkey eastwards, which may not be valid.

Danubian Bleak
Chalcalburnus chalcoides

Family name Cyprinidae (carps and minnows)
Length maximum 30cm (12in); usually up to 25cm (9¾in)

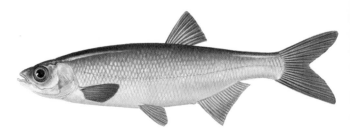

Identification A slender-bodied fish closely resembling the bleak with a small head, oblique mouth and prominent lower jaw. The body is compressed from side to side, ventrally behind the pelvic fins, forming a scaleless keel. The anal fin is moderately long based with 15–20 branched rays. Body scales small, firmly attached, 61–68 in lateral line. Coloration, dark green on the back sides and belly silvery white.

Habitat Lives in streams entering the lower Danube and other eastern rivers, also in the subalpine lakes. In many respects resembles the bleak, but this species has been little studied.

Food Believed to be plankton but also eats insect larvae and insects near the water surface. Feeds on wind-blown insects from bankside trees.

Breeding Spawns in May and June; the fish gather in the mouths of streams feeding the lakes, or in rivers migrating to shallow water with gravel bottoms. The eggs are shed in the gravel.

Range Discontinuous and not well known. Found in subalpine lakes of Austria and in the lower Danube. Also reported as distinct subspecies in the basins of the Black and Caspian Seas.

Sunbleak
Leucaspius delineatus

Family name Cyprinidae (carps and minnows)
Length maximum 12cm (4¾in); usually 6–8cm (2½–3¼in)

Identification A slender-bodied fish with a relatively large head. The body is covered with scales which are large, thin, and easily detached. Lateral line pored scales on the anterior 6–12 scales. Head scaleless, eyes large, mouth strongly oblique, lower jaw prominent. A sharp keel between the pelvic and anal fins. Anal fin longer based than dorsal fin; anal fin with 10–13 branched rays. Coloration, back olive, the sides and belly brilliant silver, an intense silvery-blue strip running along the sides.
Habitat A gregarious schooling fish living in still, small waters and slowly flowing rivers. Often occurs in irrigation channels where there is little current. Most common in waters with dense vegetation with occasional open pools.
Food A generalist feeder on surface or mid-water invertebrates.
Breeding Female lays strings of eggs which are wound around leaves and stems of plants near the surface. This primitive nest is guarded and aerated by the male.
Range Throughout continental Europe from France to the Caspian Sea and S. Sweden to the Alps. Drainage of marshlands and the use of pesticides in the small, still waters inhabited by this fish have drastically reduced its numbers in many areas.

Bogardilla

Iberocypris palaciosi

Family name Cyprinidae (carps and minnows)
Length 18.5cm (7½in)

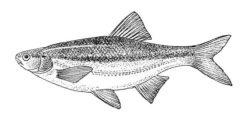

Identification A small fish from the rivers of southern Iberia.
It is relatively slender with a small head. The body is covered
with small scales, but the head is scaleless. Head pointed, with
the mouth on the lower side of the snout and slightly angled;
no barbels. Scales on the body small, lateral line curving
downwards to follow the outline of the belly; 45–53 scales in
the lateral line. Dorsal fin short based, its origin well back,
between the pelvic and anal fin bases. Both dorsal fin (which
has 7–9 branched rays) and anal fin (8–9 rays) with a slightly
curved free edge. Coloration, body brownish-green to grey,
sides yellowish, belly white; fins mostly yellowish. A dark
iridescent band from the eye to the tail fin.
Habitat Lives in the middle reaches of a river where the flow
is moderate, oxygen levels are high, together with
Chondrostoma polylepis and *Barbus bocagei.*
Food Nothing recorded.
Breeding Little studied but is believed to spawn in April.
There appears to be a great discrepancy between the sexes,
with females greatly outnumbering the males.
Range Recorded only from a very restricted area of the
middle Guadalquivir River basin. It is a very poorly known
species which is regarded as threatened.

Chub

Leuciscus cephalus

Family name Cyprinidae (carps and minnows)
Length exceptionally to 61cm (24in); usually 30–35cm (12–20in)
Weight up to 7.25kg (16lb)

Identification A thickset, round-bodied fish, with a broad head and 'shoulders'; the snout is blunt and the mouth wide. Body fully scaled; scales moderately large, 44–46 in lateral line. Dorsal and anal fins similar in shape, short based; anal fin with rounded free edge. Coloration, green or grey-brown on the back; sides silvery, ventrally white. Scales on back and sides outlined in darker colour, giving a network appearance. Ventral fins yellowish.
Habitat Typically lives in rivers especially in the moderate currents of the middle reaches, but also common in slow flowing lowland reaches and occasionally in still waters. A schooling fish when young but large specimens are solitary.
Food Very adaptable. When young, feeds heavily on insect larvae and aquatic invertebrates. Larger fish eat fishes, crustaceans such as crayfish, frogs and even young water voles.
Breeding Spawns May-June in shallow water over plants and gravel. The eggs stick to plants and hatch in 8–10 days.
Range Widely distributed throughout Europe except the extreme N. Lives from Wales eastwards to the Urals and S. Sweden to Spain, Greece and N. Turkey.

Ide
Leuciscus idus

Family name Cyprinidae (carps and minnows)
Length exceptionally to 1.0m (3ft 3in); usually up to
43cm (17in)
Weight about 4kg (8lb 12oz)

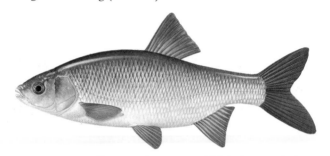

Identification Moderately slender bodied, but with a broad
head and back. Snout blunt, mouth slightly oblique and
relatively large. Body covered with relatively small scales,
56–61 in the lateral line. Dorsal and anal fins short based; the
anal fin with a concave edge. Coloration, greenish-brown on
back and upper sides, the sides silvery to white on the belly.
Pelvic and anal fins reddish. The ornamental golden orfe is the
same species.
Habitat Lives in the lower reaches of large rivers even down
to the estuarine region. Common in lower flood plain lakes. It
lives in schools in clean deep water.
Food Young fish eat planktonic crustaceans. As they grow
they feed increasingly on insect larvae, crustaceans and
molluscs, and large specimens will eat young fishes.
Breeding Spawns in April and May in shallow water over
sandy and gravel areas, the eggs sticking to weeds and stones.
Range As a native fish it is distributed from S. Sweden and
Germany eastwards to the central USSR. In eastern Europe it
is valuable commercially but is now rarer owing to pollution of
lower water courses. Its golden form is widely kept in garden
ponds and other ornamental waters.

Dace
Leuciscus leuciscus

Family name Cyprinidae (carps and minnows)
Length exceptionally to 30cm (12in); usually between
15–25cm (6–9¾in)
Weight about 0.6kg (1lb 5oz)

Identification Slim bodied with a relatively small head and
mouth. The body is fully scaled, the lateral line curving
downwards to follow the outline of the belly, with 48–51 pored
scales. The origin of the dorsal fin is directly above the pelvics.
Anal fin short based, with 8–9 branched rays, outline concave.
Coloration, greenish-olive on the back, the sides conspicuously
silvery, whitish below. Dorsal and tail fins greyish; pectoral,
pelvic and anal fins yellow to pale orange. Iris of the eye
yellowish.
Habitat Typically found in the middle reaches of rivers and
upstream in brooks. Usually found in moderately clean
running water, but, being very adaptable, may also occur in
slow-flowing lowland rivers.
Food Eats insects, both flying and in their larval aquatic
stages; takes large numbers of small arthropods which fall into
the water from bankside trees and vegetation.
Breeding Spawns early in spring, usually in shallow water
below riffles. The eggs are small, pale orange in colour and
drop between the stones of the gravel. They take up to 25 days
to hatch.
Range From the British Isles (introduced in Ireland)
eastwards to Siberia; and from Finland south to the Alps.

'Balkan Dace'

Leuciscus svallize

Family name Cyprinidae (carps and minnows)
Length maximum 25cm (9¾in)

Identification Very similar in appearance to the dace; slim
bodied with a narrow, pointed head and terminal mouth. The
body is fully scaled with about 46 scales in the lateral line. The
dorsal fin is situated immediately above the base of the pelvic
fins and is higher than it is long with a straight edge. Anal fin a
little lower than the dorsal, with a straight to slightly convex
free edge. Dorsal with 11–13 branched rays, anal with 11–12.
Coloration, back greeny-grey, sides silver and underside white.
Lateral line pores picked out with dark colouring.
Habitat A schooling fish found in the smaller streams and in
clear water.
Food Eats small crustaceans, especially freshwater shrimps,
worms and insect larvae. Has been little studied.
Breeding Is believed to spawn in early spring below stony
areas where the current is fast.
Range Known only from the rivers running into the Adriatic
Sea. It is thus found in Yugoslavia and Albania. However,
there is great uncertainty concerning the species status of these
Balkan relatives of the dace. In addition river management
(construction of dams, etc.) has greatly reduced the native fish
fauna.

Soufie

Leuciscus souffia

Family name Cyprinidae (carps and minnows)
Length maximum 25cm (9¾in); usually 12–15cm (4¾–6in)

Identification Similar to the dace with a slender body and small, scaleless and pointed head. The mouth is subterminal (on the underside of the snout). Dorsal and anal fins short based with straight to convex free edges. Body scales moderate in size, 45–48 in the lateral line. Coloration, grey-green to bluish on the back, the sides and belly silvery. A dark stripe along the sides, above the lateral line; at spawning time this takes on a reddish tinge.
Habitat Swiftly flowing streams near the upper reaches of rivers. These habitats are well oxygenated and the water is clean. Lives in schools over sand and gravel. Also reported from some subalpine lakes.
Food Believed to feed on insects (both adult and larvae), crustaceans and plants.
Breeding Spawns from April to July (late in this season in high altitudes); the eggs are shed in gravel.
Range Several subspecies have been described representing the isolated populations of this species. Was formerly common in the headwaters of the R. Rhône (France), and in the R. Rhine. Also occurs in the Alps and in N. Italy in rivers and lakes, and some tributaries of the Danube. Has become rare, and even threatened in many parts of its range. Its present status in most areas is unknown.

Minnow
Phoxinus phoxinus

Family name Cyprinidae (carps and minnows)
Length maximum 12cm (4¾in); usually 8cm (3¼in)

Identification A small fish with a rounded body and
rounded, blunt-snouted head. The dorsal and anal fins are
short based with rounded outlines. Body covered with very
small scales; lateral line curved downwards following the belly
outline, but incomplete with gaps in its course towards the tail.
Coloration, back and upper sides olive-brown, ventrally
creamy white. A series of dusky blotches along the sides, the
darkest near the tail. Breeding males have red bellies and black
throats.
Habitat Small streams, often high up in the headwaters and
occasionally in high altitude lakes. Most common in regions
where the temperature is low and oxygen levels high, but it is
found in small numbers in large rivers close to shallow water.
Food Eats a wide range of small crustaceans, insects
including those that fall into the water from bankside
vegetation, algae and water plants.
Breeding Breeds in spring (April–June) on gravel shallows
often below a riffle; the eggs are shed amongst stones.
Range Widespread in Europe; from Ireland (where
introduced) eastwards to the USSR, and from Finland and N.
Sweden to the Pyrenees and Alps, including the whole Danube
basin.

Swamp Minnow

Phoxinus percnurus

Family name Cyprinidae (carps and minnows)
Length maximum 12cm (4¾in); usually 5-9cm (2-3½in)

Identification A small fish with a rounded body, similar to
the minnow but less rounded. The back is relatively high.
Body covered with small scales which are more clearly visible
than in the minnow. Dorsal and anal fins short based.
Coloration, back brown with a greeny-golden sheen on the
sides and creamy belly. Sides are spotted irregularly with
dusky marks about the size of 3–4 scales.
Habitat Lives in still waters in the regions where water plants
are very dense. Most common in small pools and swamps
where oxygen levels are low, the water shallow and
occasionally acid (for example, in peat cuttings). Lives in small
schools.
Food Unselective; feeding on small crustaceans and insect
larvae and at times heavily on insects, spiders, etc. which are
wind blown off bankside vegetation.
Breeding Spawns in early summer, the eggs being deposited
on the leaves of aquatic plants.
Range Restricted to N.E. Europe through E. Germany,
Poland and the USSR. Within this area it is confined to inland
plains at the boundaries of water-sheds. Has become scarce in
many areas owing to the drainage of wetlands for agricultural
use.

Albanian Minnow
Pachychilon pictum

Family name Cyprinidae (carps and minnows)
Length maximum 17cm (6¾in); usually about 9cm (3½in)

Identification A small, rather slender-bodied fish
superficially resembling a minnow but probably more closely
related to the Balkan roaches. The head is relatively small but
the lips are thick, the lower lip being divided into three by
deep folds. Dorsal and anal fins are short based and the tail fin
is forked. Body covered with moderate-sized scales; lateral line
runs parallel to the belly. Coloration, light olive-brown on the
back and sides, creamy ventrally; back and upper sides with
small brownish spots each covering 3–4 scales.
Habitat A schooling fish which lives in shallow areas of large
lakes in S. Yugoslavia and Albania. It lives in open water.
Food Eats planktonic animals, mostly crustaceans but also
insect larvae and small insects which drop into the water.
Breeding Spawns from the end of March to June. Breeding
fish migrate to the streams that flow into the lakes and on to
the shallow gravel banks during seasonal flooding. The eggs
are shed over gravel.
Range An endemic species in S. Yugoslavia and Albania in
several of the large lakes, (e.g. Ohrid, Skadar).

Iberian Minnow

Anaecypris hispanica

Family name Cyprinidae (carps and minnows)
Length maximum 7-8cm (2³/₄–3¹/₄in)

Identification A small, slender-bodied fish with a small scaleless head. The eyes are relatively large, and the mouth opens on the upper surface of the head (the lower jaw being prominent and rounded). Body scales very small, lateral line short usually with 6–14 scales only, behind the head. Dorsal and anal fins short based, with 6–7 and 8–10 branched rays respectively; tail fin forked. A conspicuous scaleless keel between the pelvic fins and the vent. Gill rakers on the first gill arch long, thin and very numerous (about 100 in number). Back olive-green with dots of dark pigment, sides bright silver with yellowish flashes.
Habitat Lives in small streams in regions with shallow water and medium flow, particularly where the banks are overhung with vegetation.
Food Eats aquatic invertebrates, algae and detritus. The long, densely packed gill rakers are an adaptation for catching very small food items.
Breeding Nothing recorded.
Range Confined to the rivers Guadina and Guadalquivir in S. Spain and Portugal. On account of the destruction of its habitat and the restricted distribution of this fish it is recognized as rare and endangered in both countries. Special conservation action is called for.

Dalmation Barbelgudgeon
Aulopyge hugeli

Family name Cyprinidae (carps and minnows)
Length maximum 13cm (5in) (F); 10cm (4in) (M)

Identification Long, slender-bodied fish with an elongate
snout, pointed and narrow; mouth ventral with 4 barbels on
the upper lip. Body scaleless (as is head); lateral line running
along each side in a wavy line. Dorsal fin high with a strong
spine, serrated on the rear edges in the front of the fin.
Females deeper in the body than males and with an extension
of the oviduct on the anterior anal fin rays. Coloration, silvery
on the sides, back greenish with poorly defined dark blotches.
Habitat Lives in lakes and reservoirs as well as streams in the
karstic regions of Yugoslavia. Many of these rivers have
underground extensions or sources and it is believed that this
fish also lives in these underground streams.
Food Not known but the general appearance of this fish
suggest that it feeds on bottom-living organisms.
Breeding Not known.
Range Occurs only in the Karst area of Dalmatia, Bosnia and
Herzegovina (Yugoslavia). The rivers in which it lives have
been much modified in the past by dams to construct
reservoirs and this fish is now threatened. However, it is not
protected in any way. It is a unique species, its biology
virtually unknown.

Barbel
Barbus barbus

Family name Cyprinidae (carps and minnows)
Length maximum 91cm (36in); usually to 50cm (20in)
Weight up to 7.25kg (16lb)

Identification Elongate body, almost round in cross-section but flat bellied. Head pointed, scaleless; eyes rather small, set high on the sides of the head; lips thick with two pairs of fleshy barbels. Dorsal fin high but short based; strong spine in front of fin; anal fin short based and rounded. Body covered with fairly small scales firmly embedded in skin, 55–65 scales in the lateral line. Coloration, a warm greeny-brown on the back, golden yellow on the sides and ventrally; fins dark, except pectoral, pelvic and anal fins yellowish-orange.
Habitat A bottom-living fish in the middle reaches of lowland rivers. Particularly common in areas where the river bed is gravelly and the current moderate, often in weir pools. Typically most active at night, usually in schools.
Food Bottom-living invertebrates, particularly crustaceans, insect larvae and molluscs.
Breeding Spawns in late spring following an upstream migration to clean gravel beds. The yellowish eggs stick to stones, usually in the interstices between them.
Range Widespread in Europe. Native to E. England, now artificially distributed in England and Wales, throughout France, and the Rhine and Danube basins.

Southern Barbel
Barbus meridionalis

Family name Cyprinidae (carps and minnows)
Length maximum approx. 30cm (12in); average 25cm (9¾in)

Identification Body elongate with a smoothly curved back, but flat ventrally. Two pairs of barbels on the upper lip; the second long and slender; lips moderately thick. Dorsal fin short based but high with the first ray a strong, smooth-edged, full-length spine. Anal fin short based, but with the first rays long so that if pressed down the fin just reaches the tail fin. Scales moderate in size; 48–55 in the lateral line. Coloration, dark greeny-brown above with numerous black spots on the upper sides, dorsal and tail fins. Belly and ventral fins creamy-white.
Habitat A bottom-living fish which inhabits rivers with moderate flow. Generally it lives upstream of the barbel where the streams are narrower and flow faster.
Food Feeding habits are similar to those of the barbel, eating bottom-living insect larvae, crustaceans and (rarely) molluscs. However, the species living in the upstream habitats are not the same as those encountered by the barbel.
Breeding Spawns in May to July on gravel shallows after an upstream migration.
Range Isolated populations in rivers in southern France, northern Spain and Italy and parts of the Danube basin. Now rarer than formerly owing to alteration of stream flows by dams and for agricultural irrigation.

Po Barbel
Barbus plebejus

Family name Cyprinidae (carps and minnows)
Length maximum 60cm (23½in)
Weight up to 4.0kg (8lb 8oz)

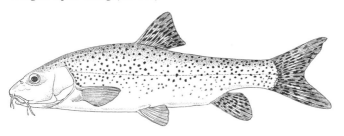

Identification A typical barbel shape with an elongate but rounded body which is fully scaled but with a scaleless head. The head is comparatively small; pointed snout with a smoothly curved forehead; eyes moderate and set high on the side of the head. Mouth subterminal with two pairs of long barbels, one at the corner of the mouth, the other on the upper lip at the front of the head. Scales small, 58–77 in the lateral line. Coloration, back greeny-brown faintly spotted with black; these spots extend on to the dorsal, anal and tail fins. Sides yellowish; belly cream.
Habitat Lives in the strongly flowing upper reaches of rivers. Rarely moves far in the river. The adults are solitary; young specimens form small schools. Most are found under large rocks or the cover of bank-side trees.
Food Mostly eats insect larvae and crustaceans, but has been found with algae in its gut. Large specimens mostly eat animals.
Breeding Reproduces in May to June, the eggs are laid over sandy bottoms.
Range Occurs throughout Italy; has even been reported from Sicily. Also reported from Dalmatia.

Greek Barbel
Barbus graecus

Family name Cyprinidae (carps and minnows)
Length maximum 45cm (17¾in); usually to 30cm (12in)

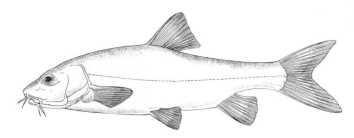

Identification A typical example of this group, with a long, slender fully scaled body, naked head with two pairs of barbels on the upper lip. The barbels on the anterior part of the upper lip are about two-thirds as long as those at the corners of the mouth, but are longer than the eye. Dorsal profile of head and body straight to gently curved. The dorsal fin is high, its origin in front of the origin of the pelvic fins; dorsal outline straight; fin base long with 12 rays, the first of which is spiny. Anal fin short based but relatively high. Scales moderately large, 50–60 in lateral line. Coloration, olive-brown on back and upper sides; laterally yellowish with golden flecks; creamy ventrally. Fins on the underside of the fish, pinkish.
Habitat Occurs in both lakes and large rivers; in the latter in the lowland reaches where flow is moderate to slow. Bottom living.
Food Not studied; can be assumed to eat bottom-living invertebrates.
Breeding Not known.
Range An endemic species to Greece, found only in lakes Yliki and Paralimni (Beotia) and the Sperchios river (Phthiotis).

Euboean Barbel

Barbus euboicus

Family name Cyprinidae (carps and minnows)
Length usually 18–25cm (7–9¾in)

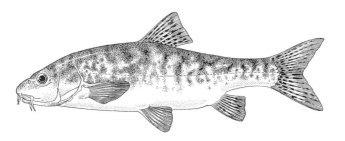

Identification This is a small barbel with a rather short body that appears deep on account of the steeply curved forehead and nape. In other respects it is a typical barbel with a fully scaled body and scaleless head, the body rounded in cross-section anteriorly but flattened from side to side. The dorsal fin origin is directly above the pelvics, the fin is short based and relatively low. The anal fin has a very short base but the anterior rays are long and the fin appears to be pointed. Mouth terminal with two pairs of moderate barbels, the anterior ones shorter than those at the corners of the mouth. Coloration, yellow-brown above, golden on the sides, creamy ventrally. A series of dusky spots on the sides form a broad but indistinct band along the midline.
Habitat Small streams; usually in the deeper pools but young ones in shallow riffles under rocks. Often found under the overhanging branches of plane trees, and under floating masses of fallen leaves.
Food Bottom-living invertebrates.
Breeding Not known
Range An endemic species on the island of Euboea, eastern Greece; closely related to *B. cyclolepis*.

Peloponnesian barbel

Barbus peloponnesius

Family name Cyprinidae (carps and minnows)
Length maximum 30.5cm (12in); usually around 18cm (7in)

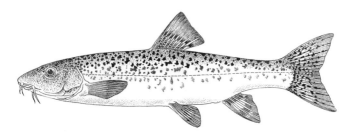

Identification A small species of barbel, which, like all
others, has a fully scaled body and scaleless head, short based
dorsal fin and a ventral mouth with two pairs of barbels. The
snout is blunt and the head broad; the lips are relatively thin,
while the front barbels are short (about half the length of the
pair at the angle of the jaws). The dorsal fin origin is in front
of the pelvic fin base; it has 8 branched rays, fronted by 3
unbranched rays (the third of which is long, bony but not
serrated on its hind edge). The anal fin is very short based and
has 5 branched rays; if depressed it reaches the base of the tail
fin. Coloration, back, warm brown, sides golden, belly creamy.
The whole body and fins covered with small dark flecks,
merging into larger blotches.
Habitat Small streams, living mainly in pools and in the
deeper rivers. Often found under the roots of trees in the river
banks.
Food Small invertebrates.
Breeding Spawns in May and June; poorly known otherwise.
Range Widely distributed in western and central Greece; also
found in Albania and Yugoslavia.

Thracian Barbel

Barbus cyclolepis

Family name Cyprinidae (carps and minnows)
Length maximum 35cm (13¾in); usually 25cm (10in)

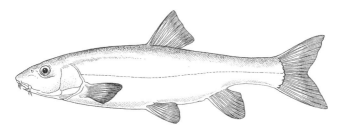

Identification A typical member of the family with a fully
scaled body and scaleless head. Also typical of the numerous
barbel species by having an elongate body, rounded in cross-
section, with a narrow tail and four barbels on the lips. The
forehead and nape are smoothly curved. Dorsal fin set above
the pelvic fins near the mid-point of the body; first full-length
spine not branched and strong, with small serrations on its rear
margins. Anal fin short based, rather long and pointed. Mouth
large; the front barbels near the tip of the snout less than half
the length of the rear barbels; rear barbels at the corner of the
mouth about equal to the eye diameter. Coloration, brownish
on the back, yellowish on the sides, white ventrally; the fins all
reddish-brown.
Habitat Main rivers and tributaries, usually in moderate
currents amongst stones and small boulders. Often hides
under mats of fallen plane leaves.
Food Some plants, particularly algae; mostly eats bottom-
living invertebrates.
Breeding Spawns in late spring over stony bottoms.
Range Lives in eastern Greece and north-western Turkey;
numerous subspecies have been described. They may be valid.

Portuguese Barbel
Barbus comiza

Family name Cyprinidae (carps and minnows)
Length maximum about 35cm (13¾in)

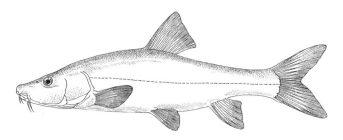

Identification Typical of this group of fishes but with a
rather elongate body and a large, pike-like head. The snout is
prominent, flattened from above and bulging at the tip. Mouth
large, opening at the front of the snout with two pairs of
barbels, the first pair shorter than the second, which originate
near the angle of the mouth. The profile of the head is almost
straight. Body wholly scaly with 49–51 scales in the lateral line.
The dorsal fin is high, placed directly above the pelvics, its
outline concave with the first full-length ray strong, spine-like
and with the rear edges toothed. Coloration, usually dull
yellowish-brown above, the sides yellowish and belly creamy.
The dorsal, anal and tail fins are spotted black; a dark band at
the edge of the upper gill cover.
Habitat A riverine species that lives in the middle reaches
and in the submontane areas. Can be found in clear, quickly
flowing streams, but is more common in cloudy, silty waters.
Food Bottom-living invertebrates, particularly insect larvae
and molluscs.
Breeding Not studied.
Range In rivers in the south-western region of Spain and
southern Portugal (Tajo, Jarama, Guadiana and
Guadalquivir).

Iberian Barbel

Barbus bocagei

Family name Cyprinidae (carps and minnows)
Length maximum 61cm (24in); usually around 46cm (18in)

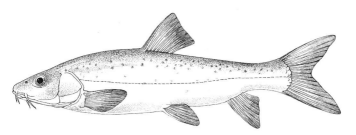

Identification Body typical of the group, long, covered with scales; head scaleless. Body seems very elongate and the head small in large fishes, but young ones have a relatively deeper body. The mouth is small and ventral with the snout prominent above: upper lip variable in thickness. The pair of barbels at the front of the upper lip are short and thin, the pair at the angle of the mouth are long. Profile of the head is steeply arched. Dorsal fin is placed in front of the pelvics; it is high with the first elongate ray heavily serrated in the middle of its length. Body scales large, very noticeable, with 46–51 scales in the lateral line. Coloration, back olive-brown, sides yellowish and belly pale yellow. In clear streams often looks silvery.
Habitat Lives in rivers, and in lakes and reservoirs along the flood plain, mostly in regions where the current is only moderate and the water clouded and warm.
Food Bottom-living invertebrates, particularly insect larvae, crustaceans, molluscs; sometimes feeds on plant matter.
Breeding May to June over sand and mud bottoms.
Range Occurs in much of Spain (except for the east) and Portugal. There is considerable variability within this range and several subspecies have been recognized.

Gudgeon
Gobio gobio

Family name Cyprinidae (carps and minnows)
Length exceptionally to 20cm (8in); usually 10–15cm (4–6in)
Weight up to 0.226kg (8oz)

Identification A slender-bodied fish with a curved back, flattened belly and rather large head. Body round in cross-section, compressed towards the tail. Mouth on the ventral surface of the head with a barbel at each corner; lips thick. Body with rather large scales, 38–44 in lateral line; head scaleless. Both dorsal and anal fins short based. Coloration, greeny-brown on the back, yellowish on the sides with a series of large, rounded dusky patches. Cream ventrally. Dorsal, tail and anal fins heavily spotted.
Habitat A bottom-living fish found in rivers and lakes. In rivers it prefers slow-flowing areas but may be found upstream in moderate currents. In lakes and still waters it is most abundant were there are gravel bottoms.
Food Bottom-living insect larvae, crustaceans and molluscs. In still waters the young fish eat planktonic organisms.
Breeding Sexual maturity is reached in the second to third year. Spawning takes place in early summer in shallow water at night, usually over sandy gravel, but on plants where no suitable gravel is available.
Range Throughout Europe; from Ireland (where introduced) eastwards to the USSR, from Denmark and S. Sweden southwards to the Alps and Pyrenees (introduced in Spain).

Kessler's Gudgeon
Gobio kessleri

Family name Cyprinidae (carps and minnows)
Length up to 12cm (4¾in)

Identification With a general gudgeon body shape, round in body cross-section and a gently sloping back and flat belly. The tail is long and slender and round in cross-section. Head relatively large; snout prominent and rounded with a ventral mouth with a long barbel at each corner. The underside of the body is scaleless; body scales moderately large, 40–42 in lateral line. Coloration, pale greeny-brown on the back but with the side conspicuously silvery with dusky blotches. Faint spots on the tail fin running parallel with the fork of the tail.

Habitat A bottom-living species which lives in swiftly flowing water, usually in the middle reaches of rivers. It requires a current of water and is not found in lakes. It is mainly solitary.

Food Little is known about the food of this species; it is certainly a bottom-feeder.

Breeding Again, little is known; it is presumed to breed on gravel shallows out of the main current.

Range A Danubian species that lives in the tributary rivers, usually fairly well upstream. It is now rare and vulnerable owing to the development of dams in these rivers, and, in places, pollution.

Danubian Gudgeon

Gobio uranoscopus

Family name Cyprinidae (carps and minnows)
Length average 10–12cm (4–4¾in)

Identification Possesses a general gudgeon body shape;
slender with a smoothly curved back and flattened belly;
rounded in cross-section. The tail is very slender and rounded
in cross-section. Head relatively small, snout prominent and
rounded; mouth ventral with a very long barbel at each corner.
The area of the throat (between the pectoral fins) is covered
with scales. Coloration, back dark brown, with a series of
dusky blotches on the upper sides; ventrally silvery. Tail fin
with conspicuous dark bars which run parallel to the fork.
Habitat A bottom-living fish which is most common in fast-
flowing stretches of rivers where oxygen levels are high and
water quality good. As a result it occurs in the upper reaches of
rivers in the grayling and upper barbel zones.
Food This is a very little-studied species. Doubtless it eats
bottom-living invertebrates which are common in the region of
the river it inhabits.
Breeding Probably spawns in late spring over gravel beds out
of the current.
Range A Danubian species which has been reported in the
upper parts of the tributaries in Slovakia, Yugoslavia, Hungary
and Romania. It is not found in the main river.

White-finned Gudgeon

Gobio albipinnatus

Family name Cyprinidae (carps and minnows)
Length up to 12cm (4¾in)

Identification Resembling the gudgeon in general body
shape with a smoothly curved back and flattened belly. The
tail is moderately long and rounded in cross-section. The head
is rather long, the snout rounded, lips thick with very long
slender barbels, one at each corner of the mouth. Scales cover
the whole body except for the throat which is scaleless.
Coloration, dusky green above; 8–10 dark blotches on the
sides, which appear bluish; lateral line marked with dark spots
in parallel with the line. Dorsal fin clear, tail fin with a single
dark stripe close to the edge, otherwise clear.
Habitat Most common in the slow-flowing deeper reaches of
rivers which have soft muddy bottoms. Also inhabits oxbow
lakes and still waters in the floodplains of rivers, and tolerates
high temperatures and low oxygen levels better than any other
gudgeon.
Food Feeds on insect larvae, particularly mud-living forms
such as midge larvae (bloodworms), and other small bottom-
living organisms.
Breeding Not described.
Range Lives in the major rivers of eastern Europe flowing
into the Caspian and Black Seas. In the Danube it is common
from the middle reaches to the mouth of the river.

Nase

Chondrostoma nasus

Family name Cyprinidae (carps and minnows)
Length maximum approx. 50cm (20in); usually 25–40cm (10–16in)
Weight up to 1.79kg (4lb)

Identification A slender-bodied fish which is compressed from side to side. The head is relatively small and the snout protuberant and fleshy, with the mouth clearly ventral. It has no barbels. The upper lip is soft but the lower lip is hard, covered with horny tissue which makes a cutting edge. Both dorsal and anal fins are short based, the latter with 10–12 branched rays. Scales moderately small, 57–62 in lateral line. Coloration, back greeny-grey, lighter on sides, turning silvery ventrally. In the breeding season the gill covers and the bases of the pectoral and pelvic fins turn orange-red.
Habitat Lives in swiftly flowing streams in the middle reaches of rivers just below the mountainous region. In larger rivers it occurs in the fast-flowing tail races of weirs and dams. It requires water of high oxygen content.
Food A bottom-feeder eating algae and diatoms which it grazes off the stones and wooden structures in the river bed. Its horny lower lip is well adapted for this type of diet.
Breeding Spawns in spring in shallow water over gravel banks in water less than 30cm (12in) deep. Spawning takes place, with a great deal of splashing, after an upstream migration from the main river into tributaries, and occurs in small schools of about 15 fish.
Range Continental Europe from western France to the rivers of the Caspian Sea, but between the Baltic Sea and the Alps. Now much less common than formerly owing to development on the rivers.

Soiffe
Chondrostoma toxostoma

Family name Cyprinidae (carps and minnows)
Length maximum 25cm (9¾in); usually around 20cm (8in)

Identification A slender-bodied fish, compressed from side
to side. The head is small and scaleless, the snout fleshy and
protuberant with the mouth ventral. From below the mouth is
curved and it has no barbels; the upper lip is soft and fleshy
but the lower lip has a hard horny covering on it. Dorsal and
anal fins both short based, the latter with 10–11 branched
rays. Scales relatively small, 52–6 in the lateral line.
Coloration, olive-green on the back, shading to yellowish on
the sides, ventrally silvery. A faint dusky stripe running along
the sides from gill cover to around the level of the vent.
Pectoral and pelvic fins yellowish.
Habitat Lives in small rivers, usually in the upper reaches of
streams where the current is moderate and the water clear. It
occasionally lives in lakes in mountainous regions.
Food Feeds on algae and water plants which are cropped
using its hard lower lip, from rocks, wooden pilings and plant
stems.
Breeding Spawns in early spring. The eggs are laid in gravel
beds after an upstream migration by the adults.
Range Lives in middle and southern France and in Spain,
particularly in the N.E. regions of Spain and also in the east.
Four subspecies have been recognized but the differences
between them are minute.

Boga (Portuguese)
Chondrostoma polylepis

Family name Cyprinidae (carps and minnows)
Length maximum 41cm (16in); usually around 25cm (9¾in)

Identification A slender-bodied fish in which the body is compressed laterally. The head is rather small, particularly in large specimens but seems larger in young fish (body length about 5½ times the head length in small fish). The mouth is ventral, without barbels; the upper lip is soft but the lower lip is hard and horny and makes a sharp edge. Both the dorsal and anal fins are short based; the anal fin usually has 8–10 branched rays. Scales moderate and numerous, between 59–78 in the lateral line. Coloration, olive-green or brownish with a dark fleck to each scale; golden on the belly.
Habitat Lives in quickly-flowing mountainous streams and in the middle reaches of river. Requires cool, well-oxygenated water.
Feeding Fine algae and diatoms which are scraped off the rocks and stones of the river bed, or off the solid walls of weirs.
Breeding Probably breeds in spring.
Range Lives only in Portugal and western Spain. To the north-west the subspecies *C. polylepis polylepis* occurs; in the southern parts of Spain and Portugal the subspecies *C. polylepis wilkommi* occurs.

Lasca (Italian)
Chondrostoma genei

Family name Cyprinidae (carps and minnows)
Length maximum 25cm (9¾in); often about 15cm (6in)

Identification Slender bodied with rather compressed sides.
The head is relatively small with a protuberant, blunt snout.
As a result the mouth is ventral, and the lower jaw forms a
straight edge. It has no barbels. The upper lip is soft; the lower
lip is hard and sharp edged. The dorsal and anal fins are short
based with straight edges; the dorsal has 8 branched rays and
the anal 8–10 rays. The scales are small, numbering 50–62 in
the lateral line. Coloration, the back is olive-brown, the
underside silvery; there is a dusky band running along the side
(starting with the gill cover) which separates the two colours.
Habitat Lives in shallow water in the headwaters of the
tributaries of rivers. Mostly it lives in small groups in shallow
pools.
Food Feeds on benthic algae and diatoms attached to the
rocks.
Breeding Spawns April to May.
Range Found only in Italy. It is most common in the
upstream parts of the Po catchment, but also lives in other
Italian rivers in the north of the country. It is closely related to
C. toxostoma, which is found in France.

Savetta (Italian)
Chondrostoma soetta

Family name Cyprinidae (carps and minnows)
Length maximum 40cm (16in); usually around 20cm (8in)

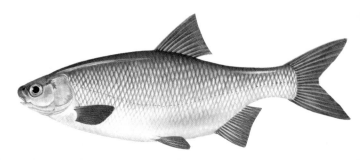

Identification A rather stout-bodied fish, the body depth
being about 3½ times the body length. The sides are strongly
compressed. The head is relatively small, the snout blunt with
the mouth just ventral. The upper lip is soft; the lower lip hard
with a horny cutting edge. It has no barbels. The dorsal and
anal fins are moderately high; both have a concave edge. The
anal fin has 11–13 branched rays; the dorsal fin 8–9 rays. The
scales are small, numbering 55–63 in the lateral line.
Coloration, the back is greyish-brown, or olive, the sides
silvery with fine dark points; the ventral fins are pale with a
reddish tinge.
Habitat A schooling fish which lives in the middle reaches of
the River Po, its tributaries and the pre-Alpine lakes on this
catchment.
Food Eats only plant material, mostly algae and diatoms with
some higher plants.
Breeding Spawns from mid-April to the end of May in small
groups in shallow water; the eggs are shed in the sediment.
Range Occurs only in the River Po, N. Italy, including the
large Alpine Italian lakes. This species is closely related to *C.
nasus* of French rivers.

Asp

Aspius aspius

Family name Cyprinidae (carps and minnows)
Length usually 40–60cm (16–23½in); exceptionally to
80cm (31½in)
Weight up to 9kg (20lb)

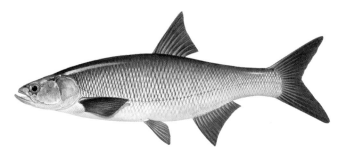

Identification A slender-bodied fish which is slightly
compressed from side to side, with a sharp keel between the
pelvic fins and the vent. The head is moderately large, and the
mouth is large, extending to below the level of the eye. Lower
jaw prominent and fitting into a notch in the upper jaw. The
anal fin is very long based and strongly concave; the dorsal fin
is high but short based, again with a concave edge. Head
without scales; body scales small, well attached, 65–74 in
lateral line. Coloration, greeny-grey on the back, the sides
silvery but with greyish scales so that it is matt-silvery, belly
white, lower fins red.
Habitat Lives in rivers, usually in their middle reaches where
the current is moderate, but also inhabits large lakes. A mid-
water fish, schooling when young but living singly as adults.
Food When young eats planktonic crustaceans and insect
larvae, will also take insects floating at the surface. Larger fish
eats other fishes, particularly the near-surface and mid-water
members of the carp family.
Breeding In April to May in running water over gravel beds;
the eggs fall between the stones. The larvae are pelagic and
drift downstream into slow-water pools. Sexual maturity is
reached at 4 or 5 years.
Range Scattered lake populations in S. Sweden. Distributed
from the Baltic states to the Caspian Sea basin and southwards
between the River Elbe and the Danube. Much rarer now than
formerly.

Ziege
Pelecus cultratus

Family name Cyprinidae (carps and minnows)
Length maximum 60cm (23½in); but usually to
25–40cm (9¾–15¾in)
Weight up to 1.5kg (3lb 4oz)

Identification A quite unmistakable cyprinid. The body is
slender and strongly compressed from side to side, the back is
almost straight and the belly is curved and extremely flattened,
forming a knife-edge. The head is short with a moderately
large and steeply angled mouth. Dorsal fin small and short
based; anal fin long based and strongly concave. Pectoral fin
long and sickle shaped. Scales small, firmly attached; the
lateral line following a wavy course along the lower sides.
Coloration, greeny-blue on the back, the sides silvery with a
pinkish tinge.
Habitat Lives in the lowest reaches of rivers and in brackish
lakes and estuaries and migrates into fresh water to spawn.
There are a few populations that live permanently in low-
altitude lakes.
Food Young fish eat planktonic crustaceans, insects and
insect larvae. Older fish eat fishes, particularly small, schooling
species such as gobies, young herring and some of the cod
family.
Breeding In fresh water at the surface and in open water, the
eggs may lodge on plants but often float downstream to hatch
in 2–3 days. Spawning takes place May–July.
Range Two separate areas of distribution: around the Baltic
basin in Finnish, Baltic states, Polish and S. Swedish coasts it
is now very rare; in the Danube and the northern tributaries of
the Black and Caspian Seas it is still fairly common.

Tench

Tinca tinca

Family name Cyprinidae (carps and minnows)
Length maximum 70cm (27½in); usually between
30–50cm (12–20in)
Weight up to 1.8kg (4lb)

Identification A thickset, heavy-bodied fish, which is distinct
from all other members of its family. Body rounded, tail deep.
The head is relatively large, the mouth terminal with a single
barbel at each corner; the eyes are small and reddish. Fins all
rounded, body scales tiny and deeply embedded. Coloration,
deep greeny-brown above with bronzy sides and a yellowish
tinge to the belly.
Habitat A still-water fish found in lakes and pools, the lower
reaches of rivers, oxbow lakes and marshy deltas. It can live in
heavily silted, densely weeded areas, where few other fishes
could survive. Very tolerant of high temperatures and low
oxygen levels.
Food Largely a bottom-feeder eating crustaceans, aquatic
insects, molluscs and a considerable amount of plant material.
Breeding Spawns in late spring and early summer, laying its
eggs amongst vegetation; the eggs stick to the plant leaves. The
eggs are greenish in colour and hatch in 6–8 days. The newly
hatched young feed on minute animal plankton, which
accumulates near weed beds.
Range Widespread in Europe from the British Isles
(introduced to Ireland and Wales) eastwards to the USSR and
from S. Scandinavia southwards to Spain, Italy and the eastern
Balkans. Because it is a popular fish for cultivation it has been
widely introduced in Europe and may not be native to Spain
or Italy. Introduced to the USA and to Australia.

Spined Loach

Cobitis taenia

Family name Cobitidae (loaches)
Length maximum 13.5cm (5¼in); usually around 8cm (3¼in)

Identification A very slender-bodied, elongate fish, compressed from side to side. The head is small, with small eyes placed high on the sides; mouth small with six barbels on the lips. A strong, double-pointed spine under the eye each side, which points backwards and is usually retracted into the skin. The dorsal and anal fins are rounded and relatively small. Coloration, light brown on the back, sandy-brown on the sides with a conspicuous regular row of rounded dark blotches on the sides.

Habitat An inhabitant of still waters and slow-flowing rivers. It lies buried under the surface mud or sand, or hides in the algal mat that often coats the bottom. It is active in twilight.

Food Little studied. Known to eat small crustaceans and rotifers; also probably nematode worms.

Breeding Spawns from May–June, the eggs being laid on algae, the roots of aquatic plants and sometimes on the sand.

Range From E. England eastwards to Asia and from S. Sweden and Lithuania southwards to Spain, Italy and the Balkans. Numerous subspecies have been described; it is probable that none is valid.

Balkan Loach

Cobitis elongata

Family name Cobitidae (loaches)
Length maximum 16cm (6¼in); usually less

Identification This is one of the largest spined, loach species, with a long, slender body. The profile of the head is steep, but the depth of the body is uniform with that of the head until past the anal fin. The caudal peduncle is long and very strongly compressed. Six barbels around the rather small mouth; the spine below the eye is small and concealed in the skin, but can be raised – it is difficult to see. Coloration, light coloured to sandy with series of dark-brown spots, those on the middle side most noticeable, but a narrower series above this, and bold marks again on the back. A very conspicuous dark spot on the upper base of the tail.

Habitat Lives in muddy and sandy-bottomed streams, rarely on gravel. Lies buried below the surface of the mud except at night.

Food Diatoms and small algae lying on the bottom; very rarely eats small bottom-living insect larvae.

Breeding In spring (May) in Romania; probably continues through June. Females are larger than males.

Distribution Confined to southern Romania and eastern Yugoslavia; probably also occurs in some Bulgarian rivers.

Golden Loach
Cobitis aurata

Family name Cobitidae (loaches)
Length maximum up to 12cm (4¾in)

Identification Has the typical loach-like slender body
compressed from side to side. The head is small; the mouth on
the underside with six barbels on the upper lip, two of which
are at the angle of the mouth. A strong double-pointed spine
beneath the eyes, but pointing backwards and usually retracted
into the side of the head. Dorsal and anal fins rounded and
short based. Coloration, back brownish olive-green, lightly
marbled with dark pigment; sides yellowish-brown with a row
of dusky spots.
Habitat Lives buried in the sand in rivers where the current is
moderate; not usually found in muddy areas. Hides during the
day but is active in twilight and at night.
Food Supposed to feed on bottom-living organisms but its
diet has never been studied.
Breeding Peak spawning is said to be in May, but may do so
from April to June. Its biology is little known.
Range Danube basin and other eastern European rivers
flowing into the Black Sea. Several doubtfully valid subspecies
have been described.

Weatherfish

Misgurnus fossilis

Family name Cobitidae (loaches)
Length maximum 30cm (12in); usually 15cm (6in)

Identification Body slender, almost eel-like and cylindrical in cross-section. The head is small, the mouth ventral with 5 pairs of barbels on the lips, the longest ones on the upper lip. Eyes very small. Dorsal and anal fins small, short based and rounded. Coloration, drab grey-brown on the back, medium brown on the sides and belly with several lengthwise stripes along the sides.

Habitat Lives in lowland ponds, the backwaters of rivers, oxbow lakes and marshes and ditches in the flood plain of rivers. It lives in overgrown, muddy conditions, which are almost devoid of oxygen and are often warm – a habitat few fish could tolerate. It breathes atmospheric air by gulping at the surface and absorbing oxygen in the gut.

Food Is said to eat bottom-living animals, mostly snails.

Breeding Spawns between April and June, the reddish eggs being stuck to water plants. The eggs hatch in 8–10 days and the larvae have long external gills by which they capture the little oxygen in the water.

Range Widely spread in Europe from France, Belgium and Holland eastwards to the Caspian Sea and from Denmark and Poland S. to Austria. The drainage of marshlands has reduced the populations of this fish throughout Europe.

Stone Loach

Nemacheilus barbatulus

Family name Cobitidae (loaches)
Length maximum 15cm (6in); usually up to 10cm (4in)

Identification Relatively slender-bodied with the front of the body rounded and the tail flattened from side to side. Head moderately large but with small eyes placed high on the sides of the head; mouth terminal, moderately large with 6 long barbels on the lips. No spine under the eye. Dorsal and anal fins short based and rounded. Coloration, greeny-brown above with yellowish-brown blotches on the back and sides; yellowish ventrally.

Habitat Lives in running water, mostly in small streams but occasionally found in larger, slow-flowing rivers and lakes. It is bottom living, hiding under stones or other objects and dense weed beds. It is most active at night. It always lives on the river bed.

Food It feds on small, bottom-living invertebrates, mainly crustaceans, insect larvae and worms.

Breeding Spawns between April and June, the eggs being shed in 2–3 batches among stones and in weed beds. The adults tend to congregate on suitable spawning grounds but do not form schools.

Range Across Europe from the British Isles (introduced in Ireland) to the Far East, and from S. Sweden (rare) to the Alps and Pyrenees.

Black Bullhead
Ictalurus melas

Family name Ictaluridae (North American catfishes)
Length usually up to 30.5cm (12in); in N. America
up to 61cm (24in)
Weight up to 0.425kg (15oz)

Identification Massive heavy body rounded in cross-section
in the front and flattened from side to side at the tail. Head
broad and flattened from above, with 4 pairs of barbels, one
on the posterior nostril each side, the longest at the angle of
the mouth (these have a broad flattened base), and 2 pairs
under the chin. Dorsal fin short based, with a spine at its
beginning; a large but low adipose fin above the tail. Pectoral
fins with one strong spine in the front of each. These, and the
dorsal spine, are only slightly serrated. Coloration, upper
surface dark-brown, sides blotchy, belly muddy-yellow; young
fish are black on the back.
Habitat Lives in still waters, the backwaters of medium-sized
streams and rivers, and in the pools formed by impoundments
of the river. Favours silty, soft-bottomed areas. Nocturnally
active.
Food Bottom-living insect larvae, molluscs, crustaceans, and
leeches which are detected by the long, very sensitive barbels.
Breeding Spawns in late spring to summer, in areas with
dense plant matter. The female excavates a nest in gravel, in
which the eggs are laid. The adults guard the eggs and later
the young fish.
Range Introduced from N. America; widely distributed in
Europe but often confused with the brown bullhead.

Brown Bullhead
Ictalurus nebulosus

Family name Ictaluridae (North American catfishes)
Length usually 20–36cm (8–14in)

Identification A stout-bodied, broad-headed fish with tail
flattened from side to side. 4 pairs of barbels on the head, one
at each posterior nostril, 2 pairs under the chin and a pair
arising from the upper lip at the angle of the mouth (these are
flattened at their bases). Dorsal fin short based with a sharp
spine in the front; adipose fin well developed on the tail.
Pectoral fins with a strong spine at the front rays. These spines
are heavily serrated on their rear edges. Coloration, back and
uppersides yellow-brown to almost black, sides brownish, belly
yellow to white.
Habitat A bottom-living catfish which lives in small ponds,
the warm bays of large lakes, and backwaters or slow-flowing
areas of large rivers on sandy or muddy bottoms. They are
most abundant in warm-water situations.
Food Feeds on the bottom at night, on molluscs, crustaceans,
insect larvae, plant matter and any edible detritus.
Breeding Spawns in late spring and early summer in a
shallow nest dug in the bottom by the adults, usually near a
sunken log or tree roots. Both parents guard the eggs and
young.
Range Native to eastern North America, this fish has been
introduced to Europe but has been confused with the black
bullhead. It is probably most common in the southern parts of
Europe.

Wels
Silurus glanis

Family name Siluridae (European catfishes)
Length exceptionally to 3.0m (9ft 10in); usually around
1.0m (3ft 3in)
Weight up to 200kg (441lb)

Identification A long, slender-bodied fish with a very broad
head and narrow tapering tail. Head moderately large with 3
pairs of barbels, 2 on the lower side of the head and the third
rising from the upper lip – this pair very long. Dorsal fin tiny;
no adipose fin on the back; anal fin very long based and low.
Body scaleless. Coloration, dull brown or green on the back
mottled with cream and yellow ventrally.
Habitat Lives in slow-flowing lowland rivers and still waters
such as lagoons, oxbow lakes and marshes in the flood plain.
The damming of rivers for navigation and extraction of gravel
has increased the number of available habitats. Largely
nocturnal in activity, it usually spends the day under overhangs
in the bank or hidden amongst tree roots.
Food Eats bottom-living fishes and also ducklings, water voles
and amphibians; young fish eat insect larvae.
Breeding Spawns mid-May to mid-July; eggs laid in a
shallow depression made by the male. Male guards the pile of
eggs until hatching.
Range Southern Sweden S. to headwaters of the Rhine;
throughout the Danube and eastwards to USSR. Introduced
to England, France, Spain and N. Italy.

Aristotle's Catfish
Parasilurus aristotelis

Family name Siluridae (European catfishes)
Length up to 1.5m (4ft 11in); usually much smaller

Identification Similar to the wels, with a long slender body, broad and rounded at the head end, tapering towards the tail. Scaleless. Head broad; eyes small; 2 pairs of barbels, 1 pair on the upper lip, the second on the chin. Dorsal fin tiny; no adipose fin; anal fin very long. Coloration, dull greeny-brown heavily blotched on the sides with lighter brown, belly greenish-white.
Habitat Lives in still water of lakes and in the lower reaches of rivers. A bottom-living fish most common on muddy bottoms. Largely nocturnal or crepuscular, lying concealed in mud or close to roots of vegetation by day.
Food When young eats planktonic crustaceans and insect larvae at the edge of reed beds or other vegetation. When adult eats fishes, particularly those near the lake bed.
Breeding Spawns in summer (June–August) in a nest created by the male; the male guards the young.
Range A most interesting species, native to the Greek river system Acheloos (W. Greece) and its associated lakes, Trichonis, Lyssimachia, Ozeros and Amvrakia. Introduced to L. Volvi (Macedonia) and L. Jannina (Epirus). Its nearest relatives live in Asia.

Burbot
Lota lota

Family name Gadidae (codfishes)
Length Up to 1.0m (3ft 3in); usually about 51cm (20in)
Weight about 0.9kg (2lb)

Identification This is the only codfish living in fresh water. Its body is relatively elongate, anteriorly rounded but the tail flattened from side to side. Two dorsal fins, the first short based, ending close to the origin of the second, which is long; neither fin is very high. Anal fin similar in shape to second dorsal. Tail fin rounded. Head broad; mouth large with a prominent chin barbel. The edge of the front nostrils extended as a short tube. Coloration, dull greeny-brown above, heavily mottled. The sides lighter, also mottled; belly yellowish-white.
Habitat Slow-flowing lowland rivers and low-altitude lakes and a few at high altitude. A bottom-living fish, which is active mainly in twilight and at night, lying hidden under tree roots, amongst aquatic plants and in crevices under rocks.
Food Young fish eat aquatic invertebrates, particularly insect larvae, crustaceans and worms. Adults eat fishes, crustaceans and insect larvae.
Breeding Spawns in mid-winter, in northern regions under the ice. The eggs are shed on the bottom and fall among the gravel.
Range Across the whole of northern Europe, Asia and North America. Formerly occurred in eastern England but is now extinct.

Mediterranean Toothcarp
Aphanius fasciatus

Family name Cyprinodontidae (toothcarps)
Length maximum 6cm (2½in); usually up to 5cm (2in);
males smaller

Identification A small, dumpy fish, with a rather broad head
and back. Dorsal and anal fins are fairly long based (10–13
rays), both are positioned well back close to the tail. Tail fin
rounded and relatively broad. Head scaleless; eye moderate in
size; mouth wide and terminal in position. Coloration,
brownish-green on the back shading to bronze on the lower
sides and yellowish ventrally. The male has a series of 10–15
brownish bands on the sides.
Habitat Coastal marshes, lagoons and drainage ditches along
the northern Mediterranean coast. Particularly common in
estuaries. Lives in poorly oxygenated, stagnant regions where
weeds and algae are abundant.
Food Not properly studied, but probably includes insect
(mosquito) larvae and crustaceans.
Breeding Spawns during spring and early summer in dense
vegetation; the eggs hatch in about 10 days.
Range Along the coastal fringe of the northern
Mediterranean, from France to Greece and western Turkey.
Also on the coastal fringes of the major islands. Regrettably the
development of coastal wetlands, particularly for tourism but
also for industry, has destroyed many of the habitats of this
species.

Spanish Toothcarp
Aphanius iberus

Family name Cyprinodontidae (toothcarps)
Length maximum 5cm (2in); the females are larger

Identification A small but plump fish with a rounded body
and short tail flattened from side to side. The body is fully
scaled; the dorsal fin is placed behind the mid-point of the
body and has 9–10 rays; it lies opposite the anal fin. Tail fin
short and rounded. The head is flattened above, the eyes
moderately large with a terminal, slightly upturned mouth.
Coloration, the males are smaller and have a greenish-brown
background colouring with 15 narrow, pale blue transverse
bands across the body. Dorsal and tail fins with a pale blue
edge but the latter has 5 brownish bands across it. Females are
also greenish-brown with rounded brown spots; the fins pale.
Habitat Slightly salt-water lagoons, pools, ponds and ditches,
often amongst dense weed cover. Such habitats are usually
warm, stagnant and very low in dissolved oxygen.
Food Eats plankton crustaceans, e.g. water-fleas, insect larve
(particularly mosquito larvae) and small snails.
Breeding Spawns in summer, about 200 eggs being laid in
dense vegetation. The eggs hatch in about 2 weeks. These fish
mature in less than one year.
Range Occurs only on the Mediterranean coast of Spain and
part of Morocco. A threatened species owing to drainage of
coastal wetlands for the tourist industry.

Valencia Toothcarp
Valencia hispanica

Family name Cyprinodontidae (toothcarps)
Length females to 8cm (3¼in); males to 7cm (2¾in);
usually smaller

Identification A relatively small and slender toothcarp by
comparison with its relatives. The body is fully scaled, rounded
towards the head and flattened from side to side at the tail.
Dorsal fin placed well down the back, slightly in front of the
level of the origin of the anal fin; anal fin relatively short. The
head is scaleless, rather small, with the mouth oblique and
opening slightly above the end of the head. Fins all rounded.
Coloration, males are greeny-brown above, pale olive-green on
the belly and sides, with 9–12 dusky, broad, vertical bars on
the sides. Dorsal, anal and tail fins are yellowish with dusky
edges. Females are paler and grey-brown in colour with a
broken dusky line running from the eye to the tail.
Habitat Lives in coastal marshes, streams and drainage
ditches in south-eastern Spain, in slightly saline water. These
waters are often overgrown with algae and other plants and
may be stagnant, warm and poorly oxygenated.
Food Eats small insect larvae and crustaceans. Potentially
useful in controlling mosquito larvae.
Breeding April–June, the eggs being shed amongst plants.
Range Endemic to Spain and found only in Cataluna and
Valencia. An endangered species owing to the destruction of
its habitat by drainage and development of the coastal lands.

Greek Toothcarp

Valencia letourneuxi

Family name Cyprinodontidae (toothcarps)
Length maximum 5cm (2in); males smaller

Identification A small, relatively slender-bodied toothcarp, although it appears to be deeper in the body than its Spanish relative. Body is fully scaled, distinctly broad at the head end but narrow towards the tail. Dorsal fin is placed well down the back, only slightly above the origin of the anal fin; both fins are rounded, as is the tail. The head is broad, rather short, and scaleless, with the mouth slightly oblique and opening at the upper side of the head. Coloration, a warm greeny-brown, darker on the back, and pale yellowish-green ventrally. Males have bright blue points on the sides, sometimes forming pale blue broken bands; females are duller.
Habitat Confined to coastal regions of the eastern Mediterranean. Lives in marshy pools, drainage ditches, and stagnant waters from karstic regions. These are often choked with algae and marsh plants (rushes), with heavy silt on the bottom, poorly oxygenated and warm.
Food Small insect larvae and crustaceans.
Breeding Breeds in early summer.
Range Coastal areas of Albania and north-western Greece (including Corfu). An endangered species owing to drainage of coastal wetlands, use of insecticides, introduction of competitors (e.g. mosquito fish). Now probably extinct on Corfu where once it was common.

Mosquito Fish
Gambusia affinis

Family name Poeciliidae (killifishes)
Length maximum 5–6cm (2–2¼in) (females);
3–5cm (1–2in) (males)

Identification Small to very small fishes with a slender body, although the female usually has a deep, flat belly. Body fully scaled; head naked. Dorsal fin short based, sited well down the body, just posterior to the anal fin base; fins all rounded. Head moderately large, about a fifth of the length; eyes moderate; mouth terminal, jaws slightly upturned. The males have the first rays of the anal fin prolonged into a copulatory organ. Coloration; pale yellowish-brown with faint flecks of brown along the body and on the tail fin.
Habitat Introduced from eastern N. America and now abundant in the coastal regions of the Mediterranean basin and inland in still and slow-flowing waters. It can tolerate high temperatures, low levels of dissolved oxygen and moderate salinity levels.
Food Insect larvae and small crustaceans. Will also eat young fish which are small enough to be captured by this little fish.
Breeding Gives birth to live young; the male's modified anal fin transfers sperm to the female, which bears up to 50 young some 30 days after fertilization. Some sperm is retained so that second broods can be produced without further mating.
Range Widespread in southern Europe and abundant in coastal lagoons and marshes. A very successful fish and a dominant competitor with the native toothcarps, such as *Valencia*.

Big-eyed Sandsmelt

Atherina boyeri

Family name Athermidae (sandsmelts)
Length maximum 9cm (3½in)

Identification Slender-bodied fish with two dorsal fins, the first of which is composed of 7–8 slender, flexible spines. Second dorsal opposite the anal fin which has 2 flexible spines and 11–13 branched rays. Head small, with an oblique mouth; eyes large. Body fully scaled, with 44–8 scales along the side from upper gill cover to tail. Coloration, greenish on the back, the edges of the scales outlined with black dots; silvery-white ventrally; an intense silvery stripe along each side.

Habitat In coastal waters and in saline lakes and lagoons. A schooling species which swims in tightly-packed groups twisting and turning when disturbed. Usually keeps to open waters.

Food Eats small crustaceans and, less often, worms and molluscs. Will also eat young fishes.

Breeding Spawns between April and August shedding its eggs over filamentous algae to which they adhere.

Range Mostly occurs in lagoons and lowland lakes on the Mediterranean coastline but is also found in coastal areas inshore. Reported from the Atlantic coast of Europe in inshore waters as far north as Holland and the S. Wales coast.

Thin-lipped Grey Mullet
Liza ramada

Family name Mugilidae (grey mullets)
Length grows to 60cm (23½in)
Weight approx. 2.5kg (5lb 8oz)

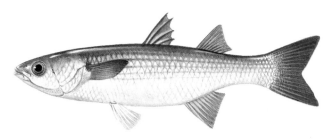

Identification Torpedo-shaped body, with a wide flattened head and broad, rounded back and 2 dorsal fins, the first of which has four strong spines. First dorsal at about the mid-point of the body; the second is midway between the first and the tail fin and opposite the anal fin. Head moderate in size, mouth wide and terminal, lips thin (i.e. narrow), eyes large. Pectoral fin short, rather rounded, if folded forwards it does not reach the eye. Coloration, grey-blue above, very silvery on the sides with faint grey stripes running lengthwise; white ventrally. A dark spot at the upper base of the pectoral fin.
Habitat Low-salinity bays, estuaries and the lower reaches of rivers, even in fresh water. Swims in small schools, often works its way over pilings and rocks grazing on mud and algae.
Food Eats algae growing on pilings and sucks in mud from the bottom to filter out small crustaceans, worms, etc.
Breeding Poorly known in this species; breeds in inshore waters; the young move into estuaries in late summer.
Range Coastal waters throughout the Black Sea, Mediterranean and Atlantic north to Scotland S. Sweden; in lower parts of rivers in this range.

Three-spined Stickleback

Gasterosteus aculeatus

Family name Gasterosteidae (sticklebacks)
Length mostly up to 5cm (2in); exceptionally to 10cm (4in)

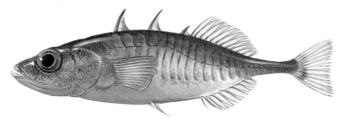

Identification A very familiar small fish with a torpedo-shaped body, flattened from side to side and with a very narrow body just anterior to the tail fin. Second dorsal and anal fins rather short and low; the first dorsal comprises 2 long spines separated from one another, followed by a short spine attached to the second dorsal fin. Pelvic fins are reduced to long, strong, rough-edged spines. Body scaleless, but some populations have a series of large bony plates along the sides of the fish. Coloration, usually greeny-brown above, and silvery or golden on the sides. Males in the breeding season have brilliant greeny-blue eyes and scarlet throats.
Habitat Lives in virtually all rivers in Europe in lowland rivers, in the marginal areas of large lakes, ponds and ditches. Prefers open water close to vegetation and is mainly solitary except when young.
Food Small crustaceans, aquatic insect larvae, newly hatched fishes.
Breeding Nests in spring and summer; the male creates the nest (a bunch of aquatic plant fibres) guards the eggs and young. Several females may lay in each nest.
Range Throughout Europe from S. Sweden to Spain, Italy and Greece; absent only from mountainous regions. Also occurs in the sea in the N. Atlantic.

Ten-spined Stickleback
Pungitius pungitius

Family name Gasterosteidae (sticklebacks)
Length maximum 7cm (2¾in); usually less than 5cm (2in)

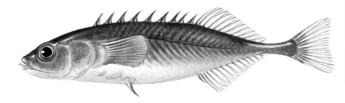

Identification Rather slender bodied with a long, thin, narrow tail. First dorsal fin comprises 8–10 short, low spines each separated from the others; second dorsal fin long based, low, opposite the anal fin, of similar shape, but comprised of normal fin rays. Pelvic fins with moderately long spines. Coloration, dark olive-green to brown on the back, lighter ventrally. Males in the breeding season have darker colours, the throat is black and the pelvic spines become bluish-white.
Habitat Lives in pools, marshes, rivers and ditches, but always in dense vegetation and on muddy bottoms. Where drainage ditches are partly choked with weeds, bankside plants and dead leaves, this is a typical habitat. It requires less dissolved oxygen than related species.
Food Eats insect larvae, small crustaceans and worms.
Breeding Male makes a nest in plants usually at 8cm (3in) off the bottom and entices one or more females to lay eggs in it. Males guard the eggs and young. Breeding takes place April–June in shallow water.
Range Coastal parts of northern Europe, from Ireland eastwards to Siberia. Not often found far inland, and irregularly distributed. Also occurs in N. America.

Greek Ten-spined Stickleback

Pungitius hellenicus

Family name Gasterosteidae (sticklebacks)
Length maximum 5cm (2in)

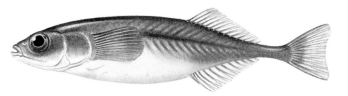

Identification Slender bodied with a very long, thin, narrow tail, ending in a rounded tail fin. Head moderately large with the mouth slightly angled and fairly large; eyes large. Head and body scaleless. Dorsal fin long based and low, composed of normal rays, opposite to similar-sized and shaped anal fin. Although in many respects this species resembles the N. European ten-spined stickleback, it totally lacks the spines on the back with dusky sides and yellowish belly.

Habitat Lives in vegetation at the edges of karstic springs and along the banks of the stream flowing from them. Hides amongst the dense rush roots and other vegetation, burrowing in the muddy bottom to escape.

Food Probably eats insect larvae, crustaceans and worms but no detailed information is available.

Breeding Nothing known; is expected to be similar to European ten-spined stickleback.

Range Found only in the basin of the Sperchios river (central eastern Greece) in springs and small rivers. Possibly extinct in some former habitats and endangered by water abstraction in others.

Bullhead
Cottus gobio

Family name Cottidae (bullheads)
Length usually up to 10cm (4in); exceptionally to
17cm (6¾in)

Identification A rather small fish, which is flattened from
above at the head end and is narrow towards the tail. Head
and anterior body flattened; a flattened spine on each
preoperculum. Two dorsal fins, both long based, the second
twice the length of the first; anal fin opposite the second
dorsal, shorter based and lower. Coloration, dark green-brown
above with very dark blotches; sides olive and the belly pale;
fins lightly blotched.
Habitat Abundant in streams, also occurring in shallow water
at the edges of rivers and large lakes, especially those with
stony beds. Usually lives under stones or in dense vegetation,
e.g. watercress beds, in shallow water, but has been found as
deep as 9m (30ft). Active at night, or when light is minimal.
Food Eats crustaceans, especially freshwater shrimps and
bottom-living insect larvae. Also eats salmon and trout eggs,
mostly those that are lightly buried.
Breeding Spawns March–May in a cavity under stones or
other hard objects; eggs attached to the underside and guarded
by the male until they hatch.
Range From England – and Wales, where introduced –
eastwards to the Black Sea; from Finland to the Pyrenees and
Alps.

Siberian Bullhead
Cottus poecilopus

Family name Cottidae (bullheads)
Length usually to 5cm (2in); exceptionally to 7.4cm (3in)

Identification Similar to the widely distributed European bullhead. Head and body flattened strikingly; tail rounded in cross-section. The preoperculum on each side has a short curved spine. Two dorsal fins; the first short, about a third of the length of the second; anal fin opposite the second dorsal and shorter based. Pelvic fins long, reaching to the vent; the inner ray is short, much less than half the length of the longer rays. Coloration, greeny-brown on the back with darker cross bars; lighter ventrally with dusky patches; pelvic fins strongly marked with cross-bars.

Habitat Lives in stony or sandy-bottomed streams and lowland rivers. Most common in relatively high-altitude streams. Hides under stones and amongst clumps of weeds in daytime, becomes active at night.

Food Bottom-living invertebrates.

Breeding Lays its eggs in a hollow excavated by the male in May–June. Eggs hatch in 3–4 weeks and are guarded by the male.

Range Poorly recorded. Said to occur from Sweden and Denmark throughout the Baltic states, Poland, and eastwards across the USSR to Siberia.

Four-horned Bullhead
Myoxocephalus quadricornis

Family name Cottidae (bullheads)
Length maximum 36cm (14in); males to 23cm (9in)

Identification A very strikingly flattened bullhead but with a relatively slender tail. The head is broad and has 3 long spines on the preoperculum and another, rather flattened one on the gill cover. Four strong, bony lumps on the top of the head, noticeably light coloured and spongy in freshwater specimens. Two dorsal fins, clearly separated, and the second with very long rays; anal fin long based and also with moderately long rays. Anterior part of the body with bony tubercules either side of the lateral line. Coloration, dark-brown above, creamy white below.

Habitat Coastal waters along the Arctic coasts as deep as 15–20m (8–11 fathoms); bottom living. Lives in freshwater lakes in the Baltic region as a bottom-living fish on muddy bottoms and under boulders.

Food Bottom-living invertebrates and small fishes.

Breeding Spawns in early winter, the eggs laid on the underside of cavities under boulders. They hatch in early spring.

Range In deep Baltic freshwater lakes (Sweden, Finland and western USSR) and in the Baltic itself as relict populations from the late ice age. Elsewhere on the Arctic coasts of N. Europe, Asia and N. America it lives as a marine fish.

Sea Bass
Dicentrarchus labrax

Family name Percichthyidae (sea basses)
Length maximum of 1.0m (3ft 3in); usually around
60cm (23½in)
Weight up to 9.06kg (20lb)

Identification Torpedo-shaped body with a moderately large
head. Two dorsal fins, the first with 8–9 strong, slender spines,
separate from the shorter-based second dorsal fin. Anal fin
similar in shape to the second dorsal. Tail fin forked. Body and
part of head with scales. Head smoothly pointed, mouth large;
eyes moderate. Two flattened spines on the rear edge of the
gill cover; a series of forward-pointing spines on the lower edge
of the preoperculum. Coloration, greeny-grey on the back;
brilliant silver on the sides and on the belly; dusky patch on
the gill cover.
Habitat A fish of coastal waters which is relatively frequent in
estuaries. Young fish in particular use estuaries as nursery
grounds and may be very abundant in mid-water that is barely
salt.
Food In rivers feeds heavily on small crustaceans and young
fish. On the coast eats a wide range of crustaceans, fish, and
even squid.
Breeding In coastal waters between March and May; the
eggs are pelagic. The young quickly move into sheltered
estuaries.
Range Coastal waters of Europe from Denmark southwards
to N. Africa and throughout the Mediterranean and Black Sea.
Young fish may be found in estuaries throughout this area.

Pumpkinseed
Lepomis gibbosus

Family name Centrarchidae (black basses)
Length maximum about 25cm (9¾in);
usually 8–15cm (3¼–6in)
Weight up to 0.481kg (1lb 1oz)

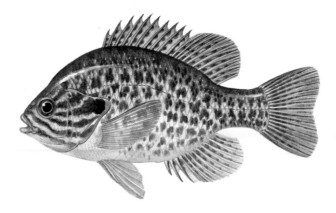

Identification A deep-bodied, laterally compressed fish with
a moderate-sized head. Two dorsal fins, the first comprising
10–11 strong spines joined to the second which is shorter and
has only branched rays. Anal fin short, with 3 strong spines
joined to the branched rays, 10–11 in number. Scales large,
35–47 in the lateral line. Coloration, back and sides olive to
golden-brown, lower sides with wavy blue-green lines,
ventrally orange; dusky bars on the sides. Gill cover with a
bold black spot near its edge but with an intense red curved
spot along the edge.
Habitat A fish introduced to Europe, which is now widely
but unevenly distributed in many lakes, ponds, canals and
lowland rivers. It favours quiet weedy bays and slow-flowing
rivers; often basking at the surface in small schools.
Food Feeds on insect larvae and other invertebrates;
occasionally takes small fishes.
Breeding Spawns from May to June; eggs laid in a shallow
hollow made by the male who guards them until they disperse.
Range Native to eastern North America; now widely
distributed in Europe, particularly southern Europe, including
England.

Small-mouth Bass

Micropterus dolomieu

Family name Centrarchidae (black basses)
Length maximum 68cm (27in); rarely longer than
30cm (12in)
Weight up to 5.4kg (11lb 15oz)

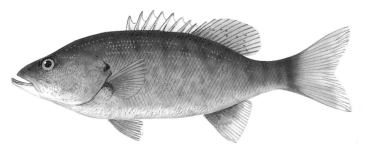

Identification Relatively slender-bodied but with a large
head, its length greater than the body depth. Body and most of
head covered with rather small scales. Two dorsal fins; the first
with 10 strong spines joined to the second, which has
branched rays; the outline of the fin has a shallow dip between
them. Anal fin with 3 strong spines joined to 10–12 branched
rays. Pelvic fins joined together by a membrane. Eye
moderately large; mouth moderate but not extending beyond
the mid-point of the eye. Coloration, back and sides greenish-
brown shading to olive green; faint dusky bars running across
the sides, and radiating out from the eyes.
Habitat In both rivers and lakes, in open water over rocky
bottoms. Tends to be a solitary fish except when young.
Food Eats aquatic insects, crustaceans, and small fishes. A
general predator on aquatic animals smaller than itself.
Breeding Spawns in May–June, the female laying her eggs in
a nest excavated by the male. The nest is usually partly
sheltered by a boulder or sunken tree.
Range Native to eastern North America; introduced to
Europe and established in a number of waters on the
continent.

Large-mouth Bass
Micropterus salmoides

Family name Centrarchidae (black basses)
Length maximum to 83cm (33in); usually much less
Weight up to 10.08kg (22lb 4oz)

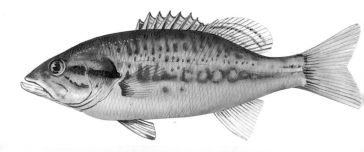

Identification Rather slender bodied but with a large head; its length greater than the body depth. Body and most of head with relatively small scales, 60–8 in the lateral line. Two dorsal fins, the first with 10 strong spines, but separated almost completely from the second by a very deep notch; the second dorsal has 1 spine and 13 branched rays. Anal fin with 3 spines and 10–12 branched rays. Pelvic fins not joined together by a membrane. The eyes are relatively large, mouth very large reaching well behind the rear of the eye. Coloration, back and top of head deep greeny-brown to dark brown, sides fading to golden-green, white on the belly. A broad almost zig-zag dark stripe along the sides, becoming broken as the fish grows.
Habitat An introduced fish. In N. America it is common near the surface of shallow lakes, shallow bays of larger lakes and in backwaters of large rivers. It tends to live in the open areas away from the dense weeds.
Food Eats aquatic invertebrates when young, but almost exclusively fishes when older.
Breeding Spawns in hollows dug by the male in March–July.
Range Native to eastern N. America; introduced and widespread but sporadic in W. Europe including S. England.

Rock Bass
Ambloplites rupestris

Family name Centrarchidae (black basses)
Length maximum about 30cm (12in)
Weight up to 0.566kg (1lb 4oz)

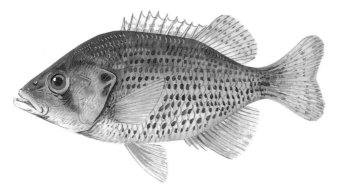

Identification A deep-bodied, laterally compressed fish with a moderate-sized head. Two dorsal fins united to form a single fin, the first 11 rays of which are strong spines. The 2 parts of the dorsal are approximately equal. Anal fin with 6 strong spines joined to 10 branched rays to form a single fin. Scales large, 37–51 in lateral line; the head partly scaled. Coloration, back and upper sides golden-brown to olive, paler ventrally, each scale below the lateral line with a dusky spot forming faint lengthwise stripes. A dark spot on the edge of the gill covers.
Habitat An introduced fish. In N. America it inhabits rocky-bottomed areas in lakes and the lower reaches of rivers.
Food Eats aquatic insects, crayfish and small fishes.
Breeding Male excavates a shallow hollow, up to 60cm (24in) in diameter, in gravel. Female lays between 3,000 and 11,000 eggs in this nest, between May and July; they are guarded by the male until hatching.
Range Native to eastern N. America; introduced to Europe but the only established population known is in S. England, where it has been living for at least 30 years.

Perch
Perca fluviatilis

Family name Percidae (perches)
Length maximum to 51cm (20in), usually to 35cm (13¾in)
Weight up to 4.75kg (10lb 8oz)

Identification Body shape variable, depending on nutrition; mostly slender bodied with a short head (about a quarter of the total length); rounded, blunt snout. Two dorsal fins, the first with 13–15 long spines, joined at the base only to the second dorsal (which is shorter based). Anal fin short based with 2 sharp spines at its front. Pelvic fins set close together, each with a spine in it. Teeth in jaws numerous but small, no large canines. Coloration, back greeny-brown becoming green on the sides and creamy on the belly. A series of dark vertical bars along the sides and an intense dark spot at the end of the base of the spiny dorsal fin; ventral fins deep orange.
Habitat Lives in lowland lakes and slow-flowing rivers, but is introduced to all kinds of still waters in which it survives but does not thrive. When young, forms small schools which gather under bridges or leaning trees; older fish tend to be more solitary.
Food Young perch eat large numbers of planktonic crustaceans, later feeding on aquatic insect larvae. Older fish eat young and small fishes (including perch) but also feed on insects.
Breeding Spawns in April–May in shallow water. Their eggs are shed in long strands which are woven around plants and tree roots.
Range Widely distributed from Ireland and Scotland (where introduced) eastwards to Siberia, from Finland S. to Pyrenees and Alps.

Ruffe

Gymnocephalus cernuus

Family name Percidae (perches)
Length exceptionally up to 30cm (12in); usually to
15cm (6in)
Weight about 0.170kg (6oz)

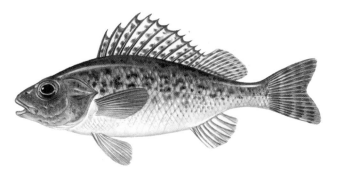

Identification Superficially similar to the perch, with a rather
slender body and short head. The dorsal fins are united to
form a single fin, the first 15 spines being long and strong, and
the branched rays slightly smaller. Anal fin short with 2 long,
thin spines at the front. Body fully scaled; head scaleless and
with large cavities under the skin beneath the jaws and the
lower gill cover. Coloration, greenish-brown on the back and
sides, liberally spotted with darker colour, lower sides yellow,
belly white. The fins are yellowish and dark spotted except for
the ventral fins.
Habitat Lives in lowland rivers and lakes in areas where the
bottom is soft mud. In rivers it occurs only where the flow is
very slow. It lives close to the bottom in small schools and
feeds both during daylight and at night.
Food Mainly bottom-living invertebrates, particularly blood
worms (chironomid larvae). Also eats fish eggs on the bottom.
Breeding Breeds in spring from March–May, the eggs stick
to plants, to tree roots, and stones in shallow water. The larvae
hatch in 8–10 days.
Range Originally occurring from E. England eastwards across
Europe and Asia, and from N. Finland to the Alps. Now
introduced to Scotland and N. America.

Schraetzer

Gymnocephalus schraetzer

Family name Percidae (perches)
Length maximum 30cm (12in), usually up to 20cm (8in)
Weight about 0.25kg (8¾oz)

Identification Rather similar to the ruffe but with a very slender body and a long, pointed head. Body fully scaled but head naked. Dorsal fin long, 17–19 slender spines in the first part of the fin, 12–14 branched rays in the second dorsal; the two fins continuous. Anal fin rather short, commencing with 2 slender spines. Body scales rather small, 55–63 in lateral line; head with large sensory cavities covered by skin on the underside. Coloration, pale olive-brown on the back, yellowish on the sides with 3–4 dark-brown broken lines on the sides; dorsal fin with 2 rows of dark dots on the fin membrane.
Habitat A bottom-living fish which occurs over gravel or sand where the current is flowing swiftly and the water is deep. It lives in small schools and forages in shallow water in the twilight and at night.
Food Eats bottom-living insect larvae and crustaceans.
Breeding Spawns in April–May; about 10,000 eggs are shed over sand or gravel in running water.
Range Native to the catchment of the River Danube; its exact distribution is poorly known. It is now much rarer than it formerly was, and seems to be sensitive to changes in habitat and water quality. Today it is regarded as endangered.

Balon's Ruffe

Gymnocephalus baloni

Family name Percidae (perches)
Length maximum 20cm (8in), usually around 10cm (4in)

Identification This is a small fish very similar to the ruffe. Its body is a little deeper and the profile of the back behind the head is concave as a result. Head moderately large, scaled on the nape but bare on the sides. A series of deep pits on the lower part of the head on each side probably have a sensory function. The gill cover has two flat spines on its free edge and 10–13 spines along its lower edge. First dorsal fin high with 14–15 strong spines; second dorsal low with 11–12 branched rays; the two fins are joined. Coloration, olive-brown above, yellowing over the sides and white ventrally. Body heavily spotted, usually forming 4–6 dusky bands on the sides. Dorsal, tail and anal fins regularly spotted.
Habitat An inhabitant of slow-flowing water, but also found in stony-bottomed streams.
Food Eats bottom-living invertebrates particularly insect larvae, and crustaceans.
Breeding Nothing known.
Range Endemic to the Danube basin. It has been captured in the delta of the river in Romania, in Czechoslovakia and upstream as far as Bavaria.

Asprete

Romanichthys valsanicola

Family name Percidae (perches)
Length maximum 12cm (4¾in)

Identification A small, slender-bodied fish, which has a
superficial resemblance to a bullhead but which is a relative of
the ruffe. Its anterior body is flattened from above and the
head is broad with the eyes on the top of the head; towards the
tail it is rounded in cross-section. Two dorsal fins, which are
clearly separated; the first fin with 9 slender spines, the second
with 15–16 branched rays. Body scales small, 58–67 in the
lateral line. Head scaleless. Coloration, back olive-brown with
dark patches irregularly distributed, sides lighter, ventrally
pearly-white with yellowish tinges. Fins yellowish with rows of
dusky spots.
Habitat Lives on the bottom of fast-flowing sections of the
River Arges in Romania. It hides under stones in mountain
brooks, probably emerging at night to hunt. It shares this
habitat with the bullhead, which it physically resembles.
Food Eats larvae of stoneflies, and probably any other of the
sparse insects of this specialized habitat.
Breeding Not known.
Range Described in 1957 when it lived in three tributaries of
the River Arges, (the Argesul, Vislan and Riul Doamnei) itself
flowing into the Danube in Romania. Now found in only part
of the Vislan. The asprete is now in grave danger of extinction
owing to dam and road construction, deforestation and the
indiscriminate use of pesticides.

Zander

Stizostedion lucioperca

Family name Percidae (perches)
Length maximum about 1.30m (4ft 3in); usually up to 60cm (23½in)
Weight up to 12kg (26lb 8oz)

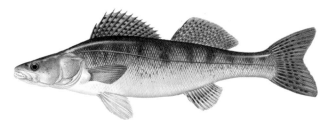

Identification A long, slender fish with a comparatively large, pointed head. The body and most of the head are covered with scales. Two dorsal fins, the first contains 13–15 strong, long spines and is separate from the second which has 2 spines and 19–24 branched rays. Both fins are long based and relatively high. Anal fin is short based with 2–3 spines and 11–13 branched rays. The head is pointed, the eyes moderately large, mouth very large (extending well past the level of the eyes). Jaws contain many small teeth and long fangs in the front. Coloration, greeny-grey or brown on the back becoming lighter on the sides and white ventrally. Young fish have a series of 8–10 dusky bars on the sides, but they become indistinct with growth. Dorsal and tail fins spotted.
Habitat Most abundant in lowland rivers and large still waters, particularly in turbid waters. It lives in mid-water avoiding weed beds and is most active in twilight conditions.
Food When young, eats insect larvae and young fish. Later becomes entirely fish eating.
Breeding Spawns in April–June over sandy or stony bottom and amongst roots of aquatic plants.
Range Originally native to the Danube system and northern and central Europe; introduced to the Rhine and to England and now common and spreading both in western Europe and England.

Volga Zander

Stizostedion volgensis

Family name Percidae (perches)
Length maximum 45cm (17¾in); usually up to 30cm (12in)
Weight about 2kg (4lb 6oz)

Identification Very similar to the zander; slender bodied and with a relatively long, pointed head. Two dorsal fins, the first with 12–14 sharp, slender spines; the second with 2 spines and 20–3 branched rays; the dorsal fin bases are so close that they almost meet; anal fin short. Jaws large, reaching back to the eye; with small teeth but no enlarged canines. Head and body scaled; 70–9 scales in the lateral line. Coloration, greeny-brown above, yellowish on the sides and paler ventrally; the sides have 5–7 bold cross-stripes, more noticeable than those of the zander.
Habitat A species which has been little studied. It lives in lowland channels and flood-plain lakes in deep water and keeps to open water away from aquatic vegetation. Hunts mostly in the half-light.
Food Its diet is believed to be similar to that of the zander, that is, invertebrates when young and fishes in later life. However, its small size and lack of canine teeth must ensure that it eats smaller prey.
Breeding Breeds April–May among stones and aquatic plants.
Range Rivers flowing into the northern Caspian and Black seas, and the lower reaches of the Danube as far upstream as Vienna. Its distribution and present status are poorly known.

Zingel

Zingel zingel

Family name Percidae (perches)
Length maximum 40cm (16in), usually up to 25cm (9¾in)

Identification A very slender-bodied, perch-like fish with a flattened underside, depressed head and long, thin tail. It has two well-separated dorsal fins, the first with 13–15 slender, sharp spines and the second with 2 spines and 16–18 branched rays. Scales on body and part of head; 82–95 scales in lateral line. Pelvic fins broad and set far apart. Coloration, back and top of head brown or yellowish-brown, sides lighter but with dark patches; belly pale.

Habitat Lives in swiftly flowing rivers in moderately deep zones as well as shallow riffles over sand or gravel bottoms. Its body form is such that with head turned towards the flow it lies tucked into the bottom without swimming effort. Most active at night when it comes into shallow water.

Food Bottom-living invertebrates, particularly crustaceans, molluscs and stonefly larvae.

Breeding Spawns from March–April on gravel beds; it is believed to conceal its eggs amongst the stones.

Range Lives in the middle reaches of the Danube and the Dniester and their tributaries. Its distribution and biology are very poorly known. Today it is a rare fish which has decreased in numbers owing to the building of dams and the excessive use of insecticides.

Rhône Streber

Zingel asper

Family name Percidae (perches)
Length maximum 20cm (8in)

Identification A slender-bodied fish with a flattened, pointed head and fairly long, narrow tail; the underside of the head and body is flattened. Two widely separated dorsal fins, the first with 9–10 slender, long spines, the second with 2 spines and 10–12 branched rays. Pelvic fins broad and set far apart. The tail is long, but the distance from the end of the dorsal fin to the tail fin is less than the length of the second dorsal. Coloration, warm-brown above; yellowish-brown on the sides with large, irregular dark brown patches. Pale yellow to cream on the underside.

Habitat Lives on the bottom of the river bed in relatively deep water, although it comes into shallow water at night. Always over gravel or coarse sand. Its streamlined, flattened body shape is an adaptation to life in fast-flowing water.

Food Not carefully studied; is probably mainly crustaceans, molluscs and bottom-living insect larvae.

Breeding Spawns March to April, burying its eggs amongst stones in shallow water.

Range Known only from the River Rhône and its tributaries. It is now very rare and an endangered species, as the Rhône has been so altered by the construction of dams and drainage channels that it is a greatly changed river.

Streber

Zingel streber

Family name Percidae (perches)
Length maximum 22cm (8¾in)
Weight about 200g (7oz)

Identification A very slender-bodied fish, flattened ventrally but with an exceptionally long, narrow tail. The head and body are scaly; there are 70–80 scales on the lateral line. There are 2 dorsal fins, which are widely separated; the first has 8–9 slender spines, the second 2 spines and 11–13 branched rays. The pelvic fins are very large, broad (and when fanned out help the fish keep a grip on the bottom). Tail (measured from end of second dorsal fin to tail fin) much longer than the base of second dorsal. Coloration, back and top of head brown; sides yellow, belly pale yellow; four sharply defined dark brown bars across back and sides.
Habitat Bottom living in fast-flowing reaches of the River Danube. It lives on clean gravel beds in moderate depths but comes into shallow water at night when it is most active. Because of its small size and slender shape it can live in smaller rivers than the Zingel. Lives in small groups in localized areas.
Food Presumed to be bottom-living invertebrates.
Breeding Breeds in April–May on shallow gravel; the eggs are buried in the stones.
Range Found only in the River Danube and in Bulgaria; mostly in small rivers. Always less common than the related Zingel, it is now an endangered species.

Lagoon Goby

Knipowitschia panizzae

Family name Gobiidae (Gobies)
Length maximum 3.7cm (1½in) (F); 3.2cm (1¼in) (M)

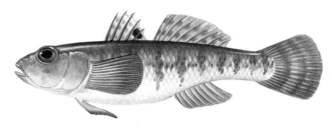

Identification A small, rather thickset goby with a deep and broad head, pouting lips and bulging eyes. The body is rounded in cross-section but is flattened from side to side towards the tail. The sides and posterior body are scaly but the back is scaleless as far back as the middle, or even the far end of the second dorsal fin. Scales quite large, 32–9 along the sides. Two dorsal fins, well separated; one anal fin; pectoral fins large, fan-like; pelvic fins united to form a single, sucker-like fin. Coloration, pale brown, almost translucent with conspicuous pale saddles across the back. Males with dark blotches on sides, extending ventrally in the front of the anal fin; head and breast dark.

Habitat In freshwater lakes in northern Italy and brackish estuaries and lagoons along the Adriatic coast. A small fish that rests on the bottom raised up on its pelvic fins and darts away a few feet when disturbed.

Food Nothing known.

Breeding Between April and August; the eggs are laid on the concave surface of cockle shells. Spawning is repeated every two weeks. Sexually mature at 1 year.

Distribution In freshwater lakes and rivers in N. Italy and along the Adriatic coast of Italy.

Canestrini's Goby

Pomatoschistus canestrinii

Family name Gobiidae (Gobies)
Length maximum 6.7cm (2¾in) (F); 6cm (2½in) (M)

Identification A small, rather slender goby, but with the broad head and anterior body common to the family. The lips are thick and pouting, the eyes dorso-lateral and protuberant. Two dorsal fins; the first comprised of slender spines, separated from the second by a small space; the pelvic fins united to form a disc. The gill cover (branchiostegal) membrane is united to the side of the throat. Scales on body rather large, 36–42 in a lateral series; no scales on the back in front of the second dorsal fin or on the breast. Coloration, pale brown to greyish with numerous, intense dark spots particularly in mature males which also have four dark vertical bands across the body, a dark chin spot and a conspicuous dark spot on the rear of the first dorsal fin.
Habitat Fresh and brackish waters of the northern Adriatic. Lives in shallow water over sand and small rocks.
Food Is said to eat worms and amphipod crustaceans but there are no reliable studies of its diet on record.
Breeding Nothing is known; probably deposits its eggs on the underside of rocks or mollusc shells.
Distribution An endemic species in the northern Adriatic; should be regarded as vulnerable owing to pollution of that sea and its outflowing rivers.

Common Goby
Pomatoschistus microps

Family name Gobiidae (Gobies)
Length maximum 6.4cm (2½in) (F); males a little smaller

Identification A small stout-bodied goby, with a broad head, thick lips and dorso-lateral eyes. Two dorsal fins, the first composed of slender spines, the second of branched rays; both fins close together at the base. Pelvic fins united to form a disc. Body scales moderately small, 39–52 in a series along the body; region of back in front of the dorsal fin and the breast scaleless. Coloration, light grey to sandy fawn with dark speckles on the body and pale saddles on the back. Mature males have a series of up to 10 vertical dark bars on their sides, a dark spot on the dorsal fin, dusky pelvic and anal fins and are dusky under the chin.
Habitat In fresh water within tidal influence in rivers and in brackish water on the Atlantic coast. Common in brackish drainage ditches and on muddy coastal marshes, but also found in high intertidal pools. Migrates into deeper water in winter.
Food Mostly small crustaceans of various kinds, worms, midge larvae and mites.
Breeding Several broods produced by each female between April and August. Eggs laid under the hollow shells of cockles and other molluscs and guarded by the male.
Distribution Atlantic coast of Europe from S. Norway, Shetland to Gibraltar and western Mediterranean.

Tube-nose Goby
Proterorhinus marmoratus

Family name Gobiidae (Gobies)
Length maximum 11cm (4¼in)

Identification A relatively large, stout-bodied goby with a
broad head and deep body. Two dorsal fins, the first joined to
the second at their bases; second dorsal fin very long based,
relatively high. Pelvic fins united into a broad disc. Head large,
its profile steep and the eyes rather small; anterior nostrils on
the upper lip form long tubes which overhang the lip.
Coloration, dull brown above with yellowish tinges;
5 irregularly shaped broad bands across the back and sides,
and indistinct bands on the dorsal and tail fins.
Habitat Lives in brackish water and in rivers within estuarine
regions. Particularly common amongst stones and in algae and
other plant beds. Always in shallow water.
Food Eats crustaceans, worms and insect larvae.
Breeding Eggs laid on the hollow underside of shells and in
hollows beneath rocks and stones. Guarded by male.
Spawning takes place from late spring to midsummer.
Distribution Rivers and estuaries of the Black and Caspian
Seas; also the Aral Sea and Sea of Azov. Now very rare in
places owing to pollution and drying up of former habitats.

Dwarf Goby
Economidichthys trichonis

Family name Gobiidae (Gobies)
Length maximum 3cm (1¼in) (males); females a little smaller

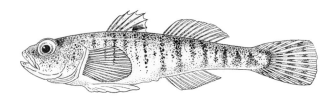

Identification A very small goby, which has the general
thickset appearance of gobies generally. The head is broad;
head and anterior body are rounded and 'tubby' but the tail is
flattened from side to side. Two dorsal fins, the first a little
more than half the size of the second, which has 10–11 rays;
anal fin similar in size (9–10 branched rays). Pelvic fins united
to form a disc. Body scaleless except for a series of well-spaced
scales along the midline of the sides and small patches on the
sides of the body behind the pectoral fins and on the sides of
the tail. Coloration, pale sandy colour with a dusky head and
back and a series of narrow dark bars along the sides running
across most of the body depth.
Habitat Lives in very small, shallow streams running into
Lake Trichonis, most abundant near the mouth of the stream,
close to the sandy or stony bottom. Lives in loose schools.
Food Not studied; probably small crustaceans and aquatic
insects.
Breeding Not known.
Range Occurs only in the region of Lake Trichonis, in the
upstream region of the River Acheloos, western Greece. It has
only recently been discovered, and must be regarded as a
vulnerable fish on account of the use of its native streams for
trout farms, and water abstraction in the area.

Louros Goby

Economidichthys pygmaeus

Family name Gobiidae (Gobies)
Length maximum 5.4cm ($1^1/_{10}$in) (F); 5.1cm (2in) (M)

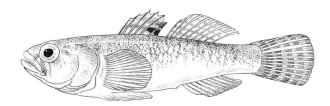

Identification A very small goby that has the general thickset appearance of the group, with a broad head, rounded anterior body and laterally flattened tail. Two dorsal fins, slightly higher in males than females; the first with 7 unbranched rays, the second with 9–11 branched rays. The anal fin is similar in shape, with 8–9 branched rays. Pelvic fins united to form a disc. Body covered with small scales from the pectoral fin base to the tail; only the back (as far as the second dorsal fin) and the belly are scaleless; 30–8 scales in the lateral line.
Coloration, the body is dusky with faint dark bars irregularly spaced along the back and sides but not below the midline of the sides. Dorsal fins with indistinct dark bars.
Habitat Lives in medium-sized rivers and streams, usually away from the main current, in areas where there is abundant vegetation and detritus. It is also present in at least one large lake.
Food Not studied; probably small crustaceans and insect larvae.
Breeding Not studied. This species (and *E. trichonis*) have a large flattened organ just in front of the anus, which may function in breeding. This organ is unique to these species.
Range Rivers of western Greece (Louros, Arahthos and Vlyho) and Lake Trichonis.

Monkey Goby
Neogobius fluviatilis

Family name Gobiidae (Gobies)
Length maximum 20cm (8in)

Identification A large goby with a stout body and rather
pointed head. Two dorsal fins, both high, and the second fin
long based; the two fins just meet. Pelvic fins united into a
broad disc with the anterior membrane with small rounded
lobes. Anal fin long based but not so high as the dorsal fins.
Head relatively long but not very wide (its width about equal
to its depth) but it is pointed. The mouth is steeply angled and
only reaches half-way to the level of the eyes; the lips are
relatively thin. Coloration, pale sandy brown with darker
marbling on the back and dorsal fins; breeding males are very
dark, almost black, with the edges of the dorsal, tail and anal
fins yellowish-orange.
Habitat In low-salinity areas, especially estuaries and
brackish lagoons on both sand and mud. Penetrates larger
rivers in almost fresh water.
Food Small crustaceans, polychaetes and molluscs; in low
salinity areas small fishes and midge larvae.
Breeding Late spring to summer. The eggs are laid on stones
and aquatic plants, mostly algae. Most fish are mature at
2 years.
Distribution Black Sea, Sea of Azov and Caspian Sea and
tributary rivers, especially the marshy estuary of the Danube.
Now much rarer in places, owing to pollution.

Freshwater Blenny

Salaria fluviatilis

Family name Blenniidae (blennies)
Length maximum 15cm (6in); usually 6–8cm (2½–3¼in)

Identification This is a relatively small fish with a slippery, scaleless skin. Its head has a steep profile, the mouth is moderate in size with slightly fleshy lips. There is a row of quite strong teeth in both jaws with a large canine tooth at the end of the row, in the corner of the jaws. The dorsal fin is long, running from just past the head almost to the tail; the anal fin is also rather long; both are of uniform height. The pelvic fins each comprise 2 long, finger-like rays (the fish raises itself up off the bottom on these slender fins).

Habitat Lives in fresh water (this is the only fresh water blenny in Europe, although 20 or so species live in the sea), in lakes and in large rivers, but not in fast-flowing areas. It prefers waters with a rocky bottom and habitually perches on the top of rocks, apparently so as to get a better view.

Food Eats crustaceans and insect larvae; occasionally small fishes.

Breeding Lays its eggs under stones in mini-caves that are guarded by the male. Breeds from April to June.

Distribution In suitable rivers along the coasts of Spain, S. France, Italy, Greece and Turkey. It is most common in lowland lakes within these areas.

Flounder
Pleuronectes flesus

Family name Pleuronestidae (right-eyed flatfishes)
Length up to 51cm (20in) in the sea; in fresh water to 20cm (8in)
Weight about 3kg (6lb 10oz)

Identification The only species of flatfish to be found in
fresh water in Europe. Its distinguishing features are as
follows: both eyes on the right side of the head, that is if laid
down coloured side uppermost with the vent towards you, the
eyes are on the right of the observer. In some areas up to 30
per cent of flounders are 'reversed', that is, their eyes are on
the left side, and the body is coloured on the left side. There is
a line of sharp prickles along the base of the dorsal and anal
fins, partly embedded in the skin; a similar patch above the
pectoral fin.
Habitat The flounder is a marine fish that breeds in relatively
shallow water on the coast. The young fish migrate inshore
and move into rivers, migrating upstream into fresh water. In
northern parts of Europe they ascend further upstream than
they do in the warmer south. They live on the river bed except
when migrating, when they swim in midwater.
Food Bottom-living invertebrates, particularly small
crustaceans, insect larvae, worms and sometimes molluscs.
Breeding In spring, in the sea at 25–40m (14–22 fathoms).
Distribution In the sea from northern Norway southwards to
Morocco and throughout the Mediterranean and Black Sea. In
fresh water it is found in only the northern parts of this range.

Index

RSNC

The Royal Society for Nature Conservation is pleased to endorse these excellent, fully illustrated pocket guide books which provide invaluable information on the wildlife of Britain and Europe. Royalties from each book sold will go to help the RSNC's network of 48 Wildlife Trusts and over 50 Urban Wildlife Groups, all working to protect rare and endangered wildlife and threatened habitats. The RSNC and the Wildlife Trusts have a combined membership of 184,000 and look after over 1800 nature reserves. If you would like to find out more, please contact RSNC, The Green, Whitham Park, Lincoln LN5 7NR. Telephone 0522 752326.